UNDERSTANDING SUPERNATURAL DREAMS
According to the Bible
A Living Classic
by
David A. Castro

Understanding Supernatural Dreams According to the Bible

Cover art: *Jacob's Ladder* (Genesis 28:10-12)
Copyright © 1994 by David A. Castro

Published by: *Anointed Publications,* David A. Castro Ministries
P.O. Box 060126   Brooklyn, New York 11206-0007

Printed by: *Diamond Printing,* Inc.
738 Grand Street   Brooklyn, New York 11211
telephone (718) 599-2500   fax: 718-782-3495

Cover Design by: *Comp U Print,* 315 West 57th Street, New York, NY
10019   telephone (212) 333-4009   teleFax: (212) 333-4034

Editorial Counsel: Eddie-Joe Irish, Nancy McRoy, Robert Sorter

Unless otherwise indicated, all Scripture quotations are from *The Holy Bible,* King James Version. Scriptures are also taken from *The Holy Bible,* Today's English Version "(tev)" Copyright © 1976, 1992, by American Bible Society, New York City, New York. Used by permission; *The Holy Bible,* New International Version "(niv)" Copyright © 1973, 1978, 1984, by International Bible Society. Used by permission; Scripture quotations marked "(amp)" are taken from *The Amplified Bible Old Testament,* Copyright © 1965, 1987, by Zondervan Corporation. *The Amplified New Testament,* Copyright © 1954, 1958, 1987, by the Lockman Foundation. Used by permission.

Printed in the United States of America

International Standard Book Number: 0-9637001-0-3
Library of Congress Catalog Card Number: 92-97483

Did Jesus Christ really promise to visit His End-Time Church with an explosion of dreams and visions? Can we expect an increase of supernatural revelations in these last days?

Does God actually plan to impart high-level strategies through supernatural dreams and visions in order to counter and defeat Satan's last great deception?

What is a supernatural trance? Why is it a "gateway" to an entire arena of other manifestations of the Holy Spirit, such as out-of-body experiences, audible voices, angelic appearances, divine sights, and other kinds of visions? Can several of these visions be found together in one supernatural experience from the Lord?

Although supernormal faith is imparted when a supernatural experience is given to us, does our own faith, knowledge, and degree of yieldedness, figure in the degree to which God would disclose that experience?

How can we tell true prophetic giftings from counterfeit ones which are demonically sourced? How can we discern whether a supernatural revelation is inspired by God, or by Satan? And if it is from God, how and when are we to apply it in our lives in a practical way?

What can we do to remember our dreams? How can we accurately interpret the many different kinds of symbols-- personal or universal ones, natural or biblical ones--which are often found in dreams and visions?

Is there anything we can do--either in our corporate settings, or in our private time before the Lord--in order to prepare for supernatural experiences?

These are just some of the questions Brother David addresses as he attempts to clarify issues involved in the spiritual realm generally, and in supernatural dreams in particular. He teaches from a strictly biblical perspective. The result is that a Bible-based faith is excited for supernatural revelations, and spiritual wisdom is imparted to properly handle them.

4

Disclaimer

In this book is found biblical knowledge and wisdom which can be a blessing and helpful to the reader. However, it is to be understood by the reader that medical, psychoanalytical, or other professional counsel is not intended here. The author is not licensed to give such counsel and does not claim to be an expert on the subject matter contained herein, but shares his observations from the Holy Bible in hopes that they may inspire one's faith in God and increase his/her understanding of the Word of God.

If professional or expert counsel is desired or required, the services of competent professionals are to be sought. The principles in this book are generalized guidelines, and should be viewed as nothing more than just that. The prayers and suggestions here are the author's own and may or may not prove to affect, influence, or otherwise improve another person's life and well-being. There may also be mistakes, as this is not the final word on the subject of dreams and the supernatural realm. Therefore, this book should be read as a source of information and inspiration, not as a source of salvation, healing, or spiritual power.

The author and *Anointed Publications* have no liability or responsibility to anyone with respect to any lifestyle change, spiritual, psychological, or physical, caused or alleged to be caused, directly or indirectly, by any information in this book.

✝

CONTENTS

SLEEP IN HEAVENLY PEACE

Proverbs 3:24   When thou liest down, thou shalt not be afraid:
yea, thou shalt lie down, and thy sleep shall be sweet.

Chapter 4   103
ADVENTURES IN THE NIGHT SEASONS
Job 4:13 In thoughts from the visions of the night, when deep sleep falleth on men.

Chapter 5   117
DREAM RECALL AND INTERPRETATION
Daniel 2:26 Art thou able to make known unto me the dream which I have seen, and the interpretation thereof?

TRY THE DREAMS WHETHER THEY ARE OF GOD
1John 4:1   Beloved, believe not every spirit,
but try the spirits whether they are of God.

Chapter 7   173
SOME EXPERIENCES
Psalms 17:3   Thou hast visited me in the night.

Dedication

To the human race, which from the time of Adam and Eve, has always experienced dreaming and sought understanding thereof...

To the Body of Christ, whom Jesus does especially desire to bless and minister unto through dreams...

To the anointed Dreamers, those chosen of God to dream dreams by the Holy Ghost...

...I cordially dedicate this work.

Acknowledgements

I would like to express my heartfelt appreciation to all my dear friends and intercessors whose prayers have made this book a reality. A warm "thank you" to Bob & Karon McGovern, George & Kristina Reninger, Danny Arvatz and his son Sal Arvatz, of *Comp U Print,* New York City, and Hector Perez and his son Hector Perez, Jr., of *Diamond Printing, Inc.,* Brooklyn, New York, for all their generous contributions.

A special thanks to Eddie-Joe Irish of *Heart of America Ministries,* Shawnee Mission, Kansas. He has been a great blessing in the editorial process, and especially in prayer. He sacrificially set aside his own publishing endeavours in order to invest two months of his life into the polishing of this book. May the Lord bless him richly for his cheerful giving.

I especially thank my own mother, Alice J. Castro, of Brooklyn, New York, with whom I lived during the writing. Her unending love, encouragement, and faith in what God could do, have always been there for me. ("Thanks Mom.") And I also thank Gabriel, the Chief Messenger of Divine Revelations, who stands in the presence of God, for all his angelic assistance.

Above all, I thank God for His faithfulness to perfect that which concerns me. *"Faithful is He that calleth you, Who also will do it," (1Thessalonians 5:24).* "Thank You, Jesus."

Foreword

Today's society is filled with many claims concerning the supernatural realm. In fact, our world currently seems to be undergoing the most profound spiritual hunger in our human history. The Body of Christ as well, is desiring to understand and enter into supernatural experiences.

Both inside and outside the Church, many people have positioned themselves to be suppliers and purveyors. The problem is not that there are no vendours peddling a variety of spiritual cuisines. The problem appears to be more of a scarcity of substantive nutrition and real food value in a wasteland of spiritual junk food. Many bellies are filled with caloric intake but little real food which can be used to fuel the furnace of the Body of Christ.

From the rivers of India to Main Street U.S.A., from the mountains of Tibet to the mansions of Beverly Hills, from the heights of the Andes to Sydney, from Mecca to Harlem and Paris, from the pyramids along the River Nile to the streets of Beijing and Tokyo, from St. Peter's Basilica to the streets of Lima, Rio de Janeiro, and Buenos Aires, from the City of David to the great avenues of London, Berlin, and Rome--our high-tech, interconnective world is a virtual supermarket of ideas, methods, and systems, good, bad, and in between, concerning the spiritual realm and supernatural experiences. So many voices, so many claims. We wonder what to believe, where to go, how to find God.

Many ungodly religions have propped onto the shelves of this spirit-market and have advertised themselves as the best product of their kind. So much for advertising. Like good consumers in any other area, we need to examine the real ingredients, not just the marketing claims.

Because of the Laodicean condition of much of the Church throughout the twentieth century, many people both inside and outside the Church have mistaken Western cultural-religionism for the true Judeo-Christian faith taught by Jesus Christ.

To preserve the status quo, the Western Church has largely been content to leave alone many valid biblical aspects of the supernatural. It has, therefore, left almost the whole arena of the supernatural to be perceived as non-Christian. Of course, certain activities are prohibited by the Holy Bible because they are not of God, and should be left alone, (Deuteronomy 18:9-14). The Apostle John said, "Beloved, believe not every spirit, but try the spirits whether they are of God: because many false prophets are gone out into the world," (1John 4:1).

In addition, the Word of God solemnly warns of and predicts the rise of the master of deception with all power and signs and lying wonders, (2Thessalonians 2:9-12; Revelation 13:11-14). Satan's masterpiece of deception will be the capture of many nominal Christians by seducing them into mysticism and spiritualism just before the Second Coming of Jesus.

Surprisingly, however, a wide variety of supernatural experiences are not prohibited by the Judeo-Christian Scriptures but, on the contrary, are greatly endorsed and set forth as desirable. The great Apostle Paul does indeed say, "I will come to visions and revelations of the Lord," (2Corinthians 12:1); and, in another place, "Quench not the Spirit," (1Thessalonians 5:19). He also encourages us to "Seek those things which are above," (Colossians 3:1).

There is a great need for wisdom to skillfully and with proper balance walk the tightrope of the permissive and the prohibitive tensions found in the Bible.

It has been said that "Satan never invents anything. He only tries to copy what he sees God doing." I believe that there is much truth to this. Obviously, then, there cannot be counterfeit revelations unless there are also true ones. Therefore, it is wrong to reject certain aspects of the supernatural just because they might seem to border on some of the counterfeit forms.

Our main emphasis is not to be on what non-Christians are or are not doing but on what the Bible says. In order to focus on the mind of Christ, we have to know what the Bible teaches. This is what this book does--it delivers a thorough, biblical approach to understanding supernatural revelations and experiences. I believe that "The correct response to the misuse of spiritual gifts is their *proper* use, not *no* use."

The great challenge, then, of the Church on the threshold of not only the twentyfirst century but a brand new third millenium a.d., is to determine biblically and accurately which is which, to discern and discriminate manifestations of God from manifestations of Satan, to try the spirits whether they are of God.

One of the greatest quests of the true Judeo-Christian faith in this hour in history is to reclaim the valid biblical supernatural arena from the domain of the cults and occults, without becoming cultish or occultish. If we are going to be successful here, we must never give in to a spirit of fear which leads to unnecessary and harmful "witch hunts" inside the Christian Church, as some have done. Nor can we, on the other hand, compromise our proper, biblical standards and cautionary guards which disdain and prohibit certain practises.

The wise King Solomon exhorts us, "Wisdom is the principal thing; therefore get wisdom: and with all thy getting get understanding," (Proverbs 4:7). In terms of the supernatural, let every student see these words again: "With all thy getting of visions and dreams, get wisdom, for it is the principal thing."

David Anthony Castro is a man of God graced with divine visions and with wisdom in supernatural things. He has demonstrated over the years, while being arrested by God for His divine purposes, the ability to walk the tightrope between the Spirit of liberty and the Spirit of the fear of the Lord; between bravely walking where few have gone before, and still upholding the old-fashioned faith of our fathers. He honours and upholds the Holy Bible's freedoms as well as its prohibitions.

I have worked side by side with David in the editorial process of this text as we wrestled to preserve both tensions and to do justice in moving toward a truly biblical guide to supernatural experiences, which have largely been lost to the Body of Christ for many years. We laughed and cried together, we prayed and saw visions together, and we have trembled and been delighted together at the going forth of the Word of the Lord.

While our respective histories in God are different in some ways, and we do not see everything identically, still it is my great pleasure to recommend not only his teaching ministry as it is presented in this book, but even more important, I recommend David as a man of God whose heart and soul is toward God and has said "Yes" in his spirit to God. He is a man of the Bible and a man of integrity. Our unity is based more on true Christian love, respect, and heart standards before God, than on doctrinal beliefs.

Is this the ultimate study on supernatural revelations? Maybe not. Someday, as the Body of Christ grows in the spirit and in understanding, a better study may indeed come along. Yet, in all my reading over the years, never have I read a better and more comprehensive presentation of what the Bible actually teaches in regard to supernatural dreams than *Understanding Supernatural Dreams According to the Bible.*

I believe Brother David deserves our respect and recognition for successfully walking the tightrope and not just barely maintaining his balance, but skillfully providing biblical balance on this much-needed subject so that others can safely cross with him.

Many years ago there actually was a brave and skilled tightrope walker who thrilled the crowds, as they came and assembled along the safe banks of the Niagara River, by walking on his high wire over Niagara Falls. After successfully crossing those great thundering waters, the man turned to the cheering crown and asked, "Who believes I can do it again?" Many hands went up, and many shouted out, "I do! Yes, you can do it again."

But the man brought forth a wheelbarrow and placed it on the thin thread of metal and asked, "Since so many of you believe, who will come and sit in this wheelbarrow while I steer him across?"

Now every hand came down, and the cheers faded away. No one had that kind of faith. The man then placed a load of bricks in the wheelbarrow and to the amazement of the crowd, proceeded to walk the tightrope again, until he had brought them safely across. Wouldn't it have been exciting if there had been just one brave soul who would have answered, "I believe in you. I'll cross over with you." The master of the wire would have carefully and skillfully carried this truest of believers safely over the dangerous falls below.

The great question before us today is not whether the supernatural exists, or whether or not the Body of Christ is to reclaim the realm of the supernatural from those who have discredited it through spurious counterfeits. Deep in our hearts, every true believer already knows that we are to redeem it. The great question before us is how to do so and how can we have the faith to do so.

No doubt there will be a few who will be content to stand along the banks and murmur against those who have the courage to attempt a safe passage. Yet that is not of primary concern. There will be others who are willing to cheer the few brave pioneers on into the supernatural realm but never think about going themselves, but that is not of primary concern either.

The great question is, "How many are willing to climb into the wheelbarrow and be safely brought across to the other side?" By these courageous ones, God purposes to build a fully purified, fully revelatory, fully supernatural End-Time Church. This is the thing of primary importance in this hour. And we say, "Do it, Lord!"

It has been a blessing to work and associate with the author in the process of preparing this book. The level and frequency of my own supernatural dreams have been increased several-fold since we began this great adventure of reading and editing. He does not teach mere theories, but with the benefit of actual experience and an authentic anointing in the supernatural. He has demonstrated ability in keeping his balance over a potentially dangerous area and in handling this wheelbarrow for others to cross with him. God bless him and all the future pioneers who will be learning to brave the thrilling but safe passage from him.

I pray that every reader will gain what is now possible to gain from within these pages--a balanced, biblical perspective on supernatural dreams. May we receive these valuable teachings and testimonies with a spirit of wisdom and a spirit of faith.

I believe that many others will have the same testimony of experiencing supernatural manifestations of the Holy Spirit. Our Lord Jesus Christ desires and has already commenced to release divine strategies to many of His people in these last days via visions and dreams. Through a virtual explosion of great supernatural revelations in these end-times, He will release higher levels of manifestations of the Holy Spirit with increasing frequency. The Lord will disclose astounding things unto us when we are properly trained on how to receive, understand, and steward them in a competent manner.

"Revelation" is about to become more than just the name of a Book in the Bible written in the first century. "Revelation" is about to be contemporized inspiration and real spiritual food, fresh manna to the generation living on the threshold of a new millenium and in the shadow of the Second Advent of our Lord.

It is my pleasure and privilege to have served as editor of this fine work, and to be a part of the team to present it to you, the reader. May it enhance not only your intellectual study, but also your own personal commissioning, breakthrough, and participation in higher realms of the supernatural. We invite you to come and eat your fill and enter the fuller realm of the Spirit of God. Come and dine, and enjoy some real spiritual nutrition. "O taste and see that the Lord is good!" (Psalms 34:8). "Blessed are they which do hunger and thirst after righteousness: for they shall be filled," (Matthew 5:6).

Eddie-Joe Irish, Chairman
Heart of America Ministries
Shawnee Mission, Kansas
August 1992

Introduction

Ephesians 3:3   How that by revelation
He made known unto me the mystery.

Mankind has experienced dreaming since the time of his creation. For just as long a period of time, he has roved in quest of hidden knowledge. He has sought the keys which would unlock the secrets of dreams and dreaming.

In this quest, man has delved into the universe of the human mind by way of psychoanalysis, hypnosis, drugs, spiritism, and religion. Because of a lack of success with these, he has even resorted to the scalpel, hoping to find the hidden things in the complex computer of the human brain with his natural eyes.

In desperation, man has often employed demonic spirits and has practised witchcraft, divination, parapsychology, and other ungodly practises. From the religious to the scientific arenas, and everything in between, man has attempted to solve the mysteries of dreaming. And after thousands of years of his existence, he has arrived at little conclusive data which can be deemed universal, consistent, or true.

Even with the vast amount of knowledge we have in this world today, the naturally-minded person cannot understand the things of the Spirit of God. They are foolishness unto him, (1Corinthians 2:6-16). Howsoever learned man may be, he is virtually helpless to understand the full spectrum of the dream mechanism which God gave us, much less to interpret dreams accurately. Any amount of success achieved by dream researchers in the scientific community may not necessarily justify a faith in their findings. As long as they fail to recognize the spiritual realm and the true workings of the soul of man, they will never understand the nature of human thought processes.

People involved in spiritism acknowledge the reality of spirits and the spiritual realm, but they fail to know the Father of spirits, the true and living God, and therefore come short of the knowledge of the truth. If they interpret a dream, reveal a mystery, or predict the future, it is only by the aid of demonic spirits, referred to in the Bible as "familiar spirits," (Deuteronomy 18:9-14).

The truth comes only from the word of God. The power

comes only from the Spirit of God. Without exception, Christians are the only ones who can be anointed of God in the area of dreams and their interpretations--or in any other area. Certainly not all Christians are anointed in this area, but only Christians can be.

When sinners experience dreams inspired by God, it doesn't mean that they are anointed. There is a difference between being spoken to and being anointed.

For many years before I was born-again, I was tormented by the devil in sleep and in dreams. I would have nightmares, would perceive evil spirits, and at times I just couldn't sleep. I think that the reason why the devil came against me in this way was because God had a plan to use me in this very area. The devil comes to destroy where God wants to bless--he sows weeds among the wheat, (Matthew 13:25).

After being born-again I gave myself to the study of God's Word. In one particular teaching tape which the Lord allowed me to listen to, a minister of the Gospel prophesied that much revelation concerning sleep and dreams would come in the Body of Christ in the end-times. This preacher said that supernatural experiences were about to increase in explosive proportions in this area. He also said great healing and deliverance were coming in this area. Along with several other verses, he referred to the following Psalms:

Psalms 3:5 (niv) I lie down and sleep; I wake again, because the Lord sustains me.

Psalms 4:8 (niv) I will lie down and sleep in peace, for You alone, O Lord, make me dwell in safety.

Psalms 127:2 (niv) He grants sleep to those He loves.

These Scriptures and the preacher's words really blessed me. I took it all in. I thought to myself, "I love this message which is comforting me. I must begin to search out more Scriptures relating to sleep and dreams."

As I began an intense study concerning dreams, in 1984, I started to enjoy sweet heavenly sleep as never before. Also, the Lord began to speak and reveal many things to me in dreams. Further, the Lord began to give me an understanding of the workings of dreams: basic dream functions, supernatural dreams, remembering, judging and interpreting dreams, and other related activities of the night seasons.

God began to use me to bless others in these areas too. Praise the Lord! Many persons for whom I have prayed, and several with whom I'm closely associated, have begun to experience dreams inspired of God. Yet I continue to pray that I may learn more about this most fascinating and crucial subject because there's always room to learn and grow more.

Revelations of the Lord in dreams and visions can exalt us. They should, for His glory. They exalted the Apostle Paul, though not above measure, (2Corinthians 12:7). God exalts us for His glory in due season and by due means so that we will fill up the measure of His purpose which He determines for us.

In the following pages, I share many of my own personal experiences in dreams from the Lord. I relate them not to bring attention to myself, but in order to teach from them as well as from God's written Word--to show how His Word applies to actual experiences. My hope is that the reader will benefit from them and perhaps enjoy like experiences.

There's a lot to learn. Nobody knows it all. But I feel it's time to share these things with the Body of Christ. And I know further enlargement will be made upon what is given here. I pray the reader will be blessed, and receive this study in the Spirit in which it is given, by the Lord.

Chapter 1

What is a Dream?

Daniel 7:2 I saw in my vision by night.

On the average, one third of our lives is spent in sleep. Our hearts and minds are awake during this time and are still entertaining thoughts. It is important, therefore, to find out how to fellowship with God at this time. We can learn what He desires of us and what He has for us through dreams during sleep.

Dreams and visions of the Lord are directly or indirectly involved in about a third of the Scriptures. Therefore, the Word of God offers a wealth of information about dreams and the sleeping state. We can understand the basic dream functions which God has created from the beginning, and thereby know what's happening when we're dreaming. We can also learn how to interpret the meanings of the different kinds of dreams we might have. Interpretations of dreams do not always require the special "gift of interpretation," but sometimes they do.

We can also define special kinds of dream experiences-- some people experience peculiar or rare forms of dreams. There are people who dream in serials--they pick up on messages they left unended in past dreams. Some people dream in panavision, others in still pictures; some dream in color, others still in black and white. In spiritual dreams, some have seen colors which do not exist in this natural world.

We often call our aspirations *dreams:* "I have a *dream,"* "I *dream* that one day..." and so on. There's a reason why we do this. We are hereby acknowledging the fact that dreams are partly meant to be visions which provide us with ideas and goals we are to set.

Proverbs 29:18a Where there is no vision, the people perish.

The Old Testament was originally written in the Hebrew language. The Hebrew word for "vision" here is *chazown,* and it means "mental sight, revelation, oracle, or dream." Inverting this verse, we can say, "Where there is a vision (revelation or goal) the people prosper," or, "With a dream, we will prosper."

Obviously goals can be set in other ways too, not just in dreams. But often during our waking hours this natural world with all its activity demands more of our attention than it deserves. This makes it difficult for us to perceive the mind of the Holy Spirit in us. In some cases, He can seldom get a word in edgewise. However, when we are sleeping, our natural functions (physical and mental) are not as occupied with natural affairs as when we are awake. Then the Spirit can more easily speak His mind.

Job 33:14-16 For God speaketh once, yea twice, yet man perceiveth it not. In a dream, in a vision of the night, when deep sleep falleth upon men, in slumberings upon the bed; Then He openeth the ears of men, and sealeth their instruction.

It stands to reason that if our enemy, the devil, can sow tares, evil seeds, while men sleep (Matthew 13:25), God can sow precious seeds while men sleep. Satan has no creative ability or original strategies but can only copy certain things which he sees God do. And he seeks to infiltrate the channel God intends for blessing, in order to steal, kill, and destroy the work wrought of Him.

A *daydream* can be considered synonymous to a *vision,* just as a *dream* is synonymous to a *night vision.* A vision operates very much like a dream except that in the former the person is awake. However, in common usage, a daydream figuratively signifies a wandering of the imagination in unreality, in fantasy, or in hopes. This further confirms the fact that dreams and visions, both day and night ones, were created to provide us with insights, goals, and ideas by which we may prosper.

One of the major differences between dreams and visions is that dreams are usually more lengthy, more detailed, and more able to progress from one stage to another. Our conscious defenses are sensitive, easily offended, and can be quite strict. While asleep, these defenses tend to relax, thus permitting the expression of thoughts and ideas otherwise intolerable.

Even in supernatural revelations written the Bible, the more profound messages usually came in a dream. These profound messages in dreams normally came to the person when he was experiencing a *deep sleep from the Lord.* When powerful messages came in visions, as opposed to dreams, the original texts signify that a trance-like experience, an angelic appearance, or a divine presence of some sort was involved, thereby overwhelming natural thoughts. As we shall see in Chapter 8, a *trance* is the same thing as a *deep sleep from the Lord.*

The more powerfully a revelation from the Lord comes, the more He overwhelms our natural thoughts. So dreams, during which our natural thoughts are already subdued, can be closer to revelations from God than day-visions.

The word "vision" is also used figuratively. As it means the same thing as a "dream" literally (according to the Hebrew: *chazown*), so also figuratively: "My love, you are beautiful as *a vision;* you are as *a dream* come true." This usage implies that visions and dreams reveal pleasant things, hence indicating that they were created for that purpose.

Psalms 126:1 When the Lord turned again the captivity of Zion, we were like them that dream.

Psalms 126:1 (tev) When the Lord brought us back to Jerusalem, it was like a dream!

"When God answered my prayer, I was so happy, it was like a dream! I thought I was dreaming! It was like a dream come true!" When the Jews were freed from captivity (Ezra 1; Psalms 126), their joy and ecstasy was such that it could only be described as a dream-like experience. This too relates dreams to desirable thoughts, again showing that God intends them for such.

In a dream, we may call things to remembrance so that we may diligently search out matters:

Psalms 77:6   I call to remembrance my song in the night: I commune with mine own heart: and my spirit made diligent search.

Psalms 77:6 (niv)   I remembered my songs in the night. My heart mused and my spirit inquired.

Psalms 77:6 (tev)   I spend the night in deep thought; I meditate, and this is what I ask myself.

It's a good idea when an important decision must be made, to "sleep on it." Tell others involved in the matter, I'll pray about it. I'll let you know tomorrow." This way you have an opportunity to inquire of the Lord and be instructed of Him in the night season. Ordinarily you won't have a supernatural dream such as Joseph, in Matthew 1:20--though possibly so. But more usually you'll have a "knowing" of His will for having allowed carnal reasonings to rest in sleep while your spirit in deep thought makes a diligent search.

This doesn't mean that we should go to bed with things on our minds. We must read the Word of God. We must pray--with the spirit and with the understanding. And if God permits, we may consult other Christians who might be able to help us cast all our cares upon the Lord, for He cares for us, (1Peter 5:7). Then, knowing all situations are in Good Hands, we can enjoy heavenly peace as we sleep. We can go to sleep trusting to awaken with the mind of Christ concerning our questions and petitions.

We have dreams so that we may seek Him Whom we love, Jesus, and His revelation, His vision, His goal. This is why man's heart doesn't rest in the night but is awake:

Song of Solomon 3:1a   By night on my bed I sought Him Whom my soul loveth.

Song of Solomon 3:1a (tev)   Asleep on my bed, night after night I dreamed of the One I loved.

Song of Solomon 5:2a   I sleep, but my heart waketh.

Song of Solomon 5:2a (tev)   While I slept, my heart was awake.

Ecclesiastes 2:23b   Yea, his heart taketh not rest in the night.

Ecclesiastes 2:23b (tev)   Even at night your mind can't rest.

The Hebrew word for "sought," in Song of Solomon 3:1, is *baqash,* and it means, "ask, beg, beseech, desire, inquire, request, and require--through worshipful prayer." The Church is to seek, and find, the mind of Christ, Whom we love, by night on our beds during sleep.

Psalms 16:7-9   I will bless the Lord, Who hath given me counsel: my reins also instruct me in the night seasons. I have set the Lord always before me: because He is at my right hand, I shall not be moved. Therefore my heart is glad, and my glory rejoiceth: my flesh also shall rest in hope.

It is through dreams that we receive much, though not all, divine counsels and inspirations to attain certain goals. And we'll rest in hope as we keep our eyes on Jesus, as we set Him always before us.

The Hebrew word translated "reins," in verse 7 above, is *kilyah,* which means "mind, interior self, and inner being." The word "instruct" here, *yacar,* means "to chastise (with blows or with words), to bind, chasten, correct, punish, reform, reprove, teach." So the Lord (by His Spirit within me) and I (including my mind) both work together for my personal instruction through dreams in the night.

The weapons of our warfare serve us here because instruction involves violent correction of the mind. It involves pulling down strongholds (arguments), and casting down imaginations (reasonings) and every proud thing that exalts itself against the knowledge of God, (2Corinthians 10:4-5). Sometimes bringing every thought into captivity to the obedience of Christ is easier done in the night seasons, (Job 34:24-25).

That's why when people are upset about something, they're often advised, "Sleep it off, you'll feel better in the morning. The sun will be shining when you awaken. It'll be a new day with new opportunities." You see, each night God will fellowship with us, inasmuch as we allow Him to, and He will even correct us. Now correction endures but a "moment," perhaps a "night." However, though weeping may follow, the joy of His favour will come in the morning, (Psalms 30:5).

It is by the wisdom of God that man is created in such a way as to require sleep. Beginning with Adam and Eve, every human being on earth has required about a third of every day of our lives to be spent in sleep. As the body rests in sleep, carnal thoughts (natural demands upon the mind) are not required, thus leaving the mind to entertain more spiritual thoughts. This is true of every human being--not just those with the Holy Spirit of God.

Marvel at this wisdom of God for a moment. Every person spends a third of his life in rest, not only from physical activity, but also from carnal thought activity. The soul is often more yielded to spiritual things during sleep than it is during the waking period.

Clearly, the sleep time is a season created by God during which man can "tune in" to the mind of Christ, if only he would yield. Or he can tune in to evil spirits, if he is not watchful enough against them, since from the fall of man the devil has been active in the earth's spiritual atmosphere.

So we see that the sleep/dream state is a spiritual one, created that way so that God can (perhaps more easily than otherwise) seal His instructions in us. When God spoke to His servant, the Prophet Jeremiah, about Israel's future restoration from captivity, it was through a dream, (Jeremiah 30-31).

In the preceding chapters, God had been speaking to Jeremiah about judgments. So changing His message into one of blessings was more easily done while the prophet was in a sweet sleep (Jeremiah 31:26), so that it may be more easily received. Jeremiah was also instructed to write the message in a book lest he let it slip away as fantasies that pass in the night.

Unconverted sinners also receive messages from God in dreams. That's why it's no wonder that many people, even the least spiritually-minded, can have significant, life-changing dreams: about their careers, their associates, their investments, and even about dangers ahead. This is also why many people, regardless of their nationality, culture, or religion, hear voices, have nightmares, or even die in their sleep. The phrase "evening of one's life" indicates that death is not far off. People are "cut off" (go up) in their place *in the night,* (Job 36:20).

The sleep/dream state is a profoundly involved spiritual arena--much more so than we realize. As Christians we have powers from God to help us operate in that arena in safety, peace, and in victory. We can understand the workings of the soul in sleep, and we can resist the forces of darkness that would attempt to visit us during sleep, (for this is, without the whole armour of God, a spiritually vulnerable state). And by faith we can learn to yield fully to the Spirit of God in dreams.

Natural dreams tend to occur more when the sub-conscious mind feels threatened, excited, disturbed, or somehow stirred. A large meal also places demands upon bodily systems--physical and mental. Hunger, another extreme, also summons subconscious thoughts, (Isaiah 29:8). Extreme preoccupations, worries, anxieties, or changes in lifestyle or daily activities can also prompt or influence dream-thoughts, (Ecclesiastes 5:3a niv).

Spiritual dreams tend to occur more in answer to prayer (Daniel 2:17-19), or in special situations, (Genesis 28:10-15). Also during a fast it may be easier to hear what the Holy Ghost would say (Acts 13:2), because our souls are then more yielded to Him.

There is a great variety of ways through which God can speak to us in various sleep phenomena, such as through trances (sometimes termed "deep sleep"), through super-natural visions, through out-of-body experiences, or through the ministry of angels. But these kinds of supernatural manifestations are occasional and not daily. Yet we may daily, and nightly in dreams, fellowship with Jesus and be led of Him. We may receive the Lord's guidance, wisdom, confirmation, and other insights and blessings, each night by His Holy Spirit in us whether or not they come in a spectacular form.

God is presently observing all activity in the earth. By His mercy He holds back most of the wrath man deserves for sin. In the Great Judgment Day it will be as though He has awakened from a despicable dream--this present time. He'll despise the wicked as a man despises his bad dreams.

Psalms 73:20   As a dream when one awaketh; so, O Lord, when Thou awakest, Thou shalt despise their image.

Psalms 73:20 (tev)   They are like a dream that goes away in the morning; when You rouse Yourself, O Lord, they disappear.

Psalms 73:20 (niv)   As a dream when one awakes, so when You arise, O Lord, You will despise them as fantasies.

At that time, on the Great White Throne Judgment Day (Revelation 20:11-12), God's wrath will be awakened against the wicked fully--100%. Man's consciousness will also be awakened 100%, compared to the roughly 10% he now exercises. (The man in Hell, in Luke 16:19-31, realized things which he didn't know previously. He recognized the Patriarch Abraham who had lived centuries earlier.) The average human mind exercises about 10-12% of its capacity in conscious thought, but will exercise 100% in the eternal home--be it Paradise, or be it Hell and the Lake of Fire.

Likewise the mind in the dream state exercises a fraction (about a tithe, a tenth) of the conscious thought processes active in the waking state. Some have said, "I had a dream that I had a dream." In a sense we can all say, "I'm dreaming now, and I have dreams in this dream."

A man's life on earth, operating with about a tithe of his consciousness, is a grace period during which he should seek the Lord's will. It is also a time during which, by certain circumstances in his life, he can see how far he is from God's perfect will. Well, since a dream is likened unto this present life (according to Psalms 73:20), a dream also is "a grace period during which we should seek, and find, the Lord's will for our lives." And it is also "a time during which, by certain circumstances occurring in our dreams, we can see where we stand as far as concerns God's perfect will for our lives."

Further, when we awaken we may behold God's presence in our real lives, much as when we awaken from this life, at death, and enter into fullness of life in His presence, (Psalms 17:15). And when we awaken we may be satisfied that He has spoken to us, and walk confidently in His will in our real lives. For at death we awaken from this life and enter into fullness of life in His reality, (Psalms 16:11).

Colossians 3:3-4 For ye are dead, and your life is hid with Christ in God. When Christ, Who is our Life, shall appear, then shall ye also appear with Him in glory.

God, through the Prophet Malachi (Malachi 3:10), commands us to give Him a tithe of all our possessions. And the tithe of our minds which He is requiring is the conscious portion--the choice part. We must continually give ourselves unto the Lord. If we give Him this "firstfruits" (for the tithe is the Lord's), there will be meat in His house.

We are the temple of the Holy Spirit (1Corinthians 6:19), and His provision will be in us. The windows of Heaven will be open unto us--while we're awake (as in eternity) and while we dream (as in this present world).

Remember, the waking state is to eternity as what dreaming is to the waking state.

Facts About Sleep and Dreams

1)   The Mind is Entertaining Thoughts During Sleep

Normally while sleeping, the mind is almost constantly dreaming, according to EEG test studies. However, most dreams are not remembered or understood. According to *Webster's Dictionary,* an EEG (electroencephalogram) is a tracing which shows the changes in electric potential produced by the brain. In other words, through EEG tests we find that the mind is almost constantly awake, working, and producing thought during sleep. However, during some very short periods there is minimal thought activity indicated--probably no dreaming at these times.

Often we can recognize when a person is having a dream. His eyelids may vibrate rapidly because his eyes are reacting to the scenes he's viewing. His facial expression or body movements may indicate that he's dreaming. At times body positions speak of what's being dreamed. Or he may be talking, laughing, or crying in his sleep, indicating that he's dreaming. However, with none of this behaviour evident, he may still be dreaming.

Everybody dreams. Every human being that has ever lived, from every generation since Adam and Eve--every race, creed, culture and religion. One of the most basic functions of dreaming is the repeating of memories. These memories may be perceptions from our recent or distant past. If we understand this, we can see why everyone dreams. Even the sick, retarded, feeble, and newborns dream to some degree, because their thinking processes are active to some degree (with the exception of those in a coma).

Animals may also dream during their sleep. In one experiment conducted to prove this, brain surgery was performed on a cat so that while sleeping his body reflexes would not be able to distinguish between his dream life and reality. Dream researchers filmed the cat as he slept and saw him doing what he normally does when awake-- running, jumping, meowing, and striking with his paws. Other animals have also shown evidence that they dream.

Animals' dreams are of the most simple sorts, because their thinking is. And the simpler its brain is, the simpler is its thinking and dreaming. We might be safe in saying, "If it thinks, it dreams," because the function of dreaming is essentially one of thinking.

People can form patterns of dreaming. One might consistently have more dreams during a certain part of his sleep and less during another part. Some people may seldom dream during light rest, but often in deep sleep. Others' patterns may be completely the opposite. These patterns may differ among people.

As the body is always active (though at times less active than at other times), so the mind in dreams is always active (though at times not very active). The fact that there is thought activity during sleep (in varying degrees of semi-consciousness) is abundantly verified throughout the Bible. The following verses show this:

Isaiah 26:9a With my soul have I desired Thee in the night; yea, with my spirit within me will I seek Thee early.

Isaiah 26:9a (amp) My soul yearns for You [O Lord] in the night.

Psalms 63:5-6 My soul shall be satisfied as with marrow and fatness; and my mouth shall praise Thee with joyful lips: When I remember Thee upon my bed, and meditate on Thee in the night watches.

2Timothy 1:3 I thank God, Whom I serve from my forefathers with pure conscience, that without ceasing I have remembrance of thee in my prayers night and day.

King David, in the Book of Psalms, often speaks of seeking and praising the Lord in the "night seasons." The

Apostle Paul in his epistles often speaks of praying and interceding without ceasing "night and day." Others also intensely communed with the Lord "day and night." (See Joshua 1:8; Lamentations 2:18; Luke 18:7; Psalms 6:6; 22:2; 32:4; 42:3; 88:1).

Repeatedly throughout the Bible we find such terms as "the night seasons," "day and night," "the visions of the night," and similar terms, associated with some form of prayer. Even though prayer during the *night watches* of the Lord often occurs while we are awake (Psalms 119:147-148), these terms can also denote fellowship with the Lord during sleep, and not just while it's night time.

So we see that God's servants in the Bible enjoyed wonderful fellowship with Him during the night seasons, and not only in the supernatural kinds of dreams. Christians today also can enjoy God's presence in sleep. Even more so, as a matter of fact, because we have more of His presence in the world in this dispensation. We are baptized into Him in the new birth, filled with His Spirit and power, and we have the full canon of Scripture which the first Christians and Old Testament saints lacked.

Also, the Body of Christ has matured considerably in spiritual knowledge and understanding during the past nineteen hundred years. We have more wisdom now concerning the ways of the Lord and can yield to Him more fully--even in the area of dreams.

Sinners who don't yield unto God, and those Christians who don't yield unto Him as much as they should, still have dreams. But their dream experiences can be (and often are) as unenjoyable as godly dreams are enjoyable.

2) Day Experiences are Simulated in Dream-Thoughts

Since the mind is active while we sleep, although in greater or lesser degrees throughout the sleep period, what kinds of thoughts do we entertain? Dream invest- igators in the psychoanalytical field have found that dreams are mostly made up of repressed personality traits (often socially reprehensible ones), the gratification of desires (often unattainable in reality), and attempts or ideas to solve problems which exist in the real life. Dreams also contain memories of the past, hopes for the future, and perceptions (often distorted ones) of present circumstances. Of course, this is a very broad generalization, and there are variables to consider. Noteworthy are these variables:

* Many symbols, both personal and universal ones, are found in most dreams.

* Thoughts of the past, present, and future, may be seen in the same dream.

* One can subconsciously edit his dreams as he pleases: while they're occurring, or after he awakens.

* While sleeping, a person can perceive physical activity near him--somebody may speak to him or touch him-- thereby enhancing, affecting, or otherwise altering the dream content.

As far as the natural understanding is concerned (which understanding dream investigators are wholly limited to), these findings are scripturally agreeable. The biblical view, however, is a more full one because it acknowledges the spiritual dimension, which has the major role in dreams. The spiritual realm is the center around which all mental and natural activity revolves.

The Word of God tells us that one of the signs of the last days is an increase of visions and dreams:

Acts 2:17 And it shall come to pass in the last days, saith God, I will pour out of My Spirit upon all flesh: and your sons and your daughters shall prophesy, and your young men shall see visions, and your old men shall dream dreams.

Men have always had dreams. But now, in these last days, we will experience more dreams than ever before because there are more words in the world than ever before, and also more activity:

Ecclesiastes 5:3a   For a dream cometh through the multitude of business.

The Hebrew word translated "business" here is *inyan,* and it means "activity, speech, employment, ado." Hence the increase of dreams in these last days, a result of the exhorbitant *inyan* in the world presently.

Also notice, again in Acts 2:17, that the prophetic word of the Lord precedes the increase of dreams in the people of God. (The *Amplified Bible* says "divinely suggested dreams.") This also confirms the fact that dreams are caused by much activity, words, and business. But if God's words aren't influencing our dreams, then the business, bustle, and ado of this world's system are.

Ecclesiastes 5:2-3   Be not rash with thy mouth, and let not thine heart be hasty to utter anything before God: for God is in Heaven, and thou upon earth: therefore let thy words be few. For a dream cometh through the multitude of business; and a fool's voice is known by multitude of words.

As a fool's voice is known by a multitude of words, so also a foolish dream is recognized by a multitude of activity in the dream. And a multitude of foolish dreams is caused by a multitude of foolish business. This is seen again in verse 7:

Ecclesiastes 5:7   For in the multitude of dreams and many words there are also divers vanities.

Having this insight, let's choose wisdom and life as the Psalmist David. He kept God's precepts during the day, and as a result remembered the Name of the Lord in the night:

Psalms 119:55-56 I have remembered Thy Name, O Lord, in the
night, and have kept Thy law. This I had, because I kept Thy
precepts.

The Name of the Lord was King David's strong tower
whereunto he continually resorted, (Proverbs 18:10). We
also, being the righteousness of God in Christ, may run to
the Lord and be safe in the night seasons. But we must,
like David, fill our souls with God's business--His Word,
His Spirit, His precepts--because what we're occupied with
during the day will show up in our night visions.

3) Physiological Factors Affect Our Dream Experiences

When a person is sleeping, his five senses are still
operating, although on a lower level of awareness and
understanding--this is the body's rest period. During this
time, the mind can, and often does, acknowledge and
interpret new information as it is being perceived by the
senses. As new information is introduced, new thoughts,
impressions, words, or pictures can be added into the
dream messages and can thereby alter them.

Based on this fact, we can have certain anointed music
or Bible teaching tapes playing as we sleep and allow them
to influence our dreams for good. I've done this many
times and have enjoyed wonderful sleep as a result. Often
the words and music I heard were not really on the tapes.
The taped message would become altered and my mind
would receive the message I needed to hear. The preacher
on the tape would even look at me and prophesy the
accurate word of the Lord unto me.

A couple of times I have fallen asleep on my sofa while
viewing Christian programs on television, and dreamed I
was on some of those programs fellowshipping with the
brethren there. In those influenced dreams, I would have
prophetic words of knowledge and of wisdom for some of

them, and they would have some for me.

This shouldn't be a surprising revelation. This is a well-known fact, if we would only think about it. Consider for a moment the negative side of this truth. If a person falls asleep with ungodly music playing, or in front of the television while a horror movie or some other ungodly program is playing, it's understandable that they can have a bad dream or a nightmare as a result. The devil tries to take advantage of every opportunity a person gives him to torment them, particularly at such vulnerable times as during sleep.

The psychospiritual principle of receiving suggestions during a semi-conscious state--when a person is not completely awake or alert--is well taken advantage of by many people who practise non-Christian meditation techniques such as hypnosis, mind control, transcendental meditation, and other doctrines of devils. Yet the principle itself is not devilish. It is simply a natural function of the mind which can be used for one's benefit.

These people realize that subliminal suggestions are provided through their teaching tapes as they sleep--often more so than when they're awake--to help them improve their lives. And to some degree there may indeed be an improvement: such as healthier habits, financial prosperity, a better self-image, etc. But what they don't realize is that when they thus open up their spirits to suggestions which do not glorify Jesus Christ, the Holy Spirit of God is not involved, because the Holy Spirit is sent for the purpose of testifying of and glorifying Jesus Christ, (John 15:26; 16:13-14).

Therefore, being spiritually open and receptive without God, evil spirits can begin to have access in their lives more than ever before. And in time it becomes easier to believe in Satan's lies: secular humanism, abortion, homosexuality, body worship, and eventually eastern mysticism, astrology, witchcraft, and Satan worship.

So we can see the danger in yielding our spirits to subliminal suggestions without God. But it is equally beneficial if we do so with God. Reading the Bible regularly, making confessions of faith, and listening to anointed music and teaching tapes--all to the glory of Jesus--can be done while we're awake and while we're asleep. And this helps us in believing and understanding the truths of God.

As Christians, we would be wise not to place too much emphasis on this. Let's not go to extremes and play certain tapes every night ritualistically. It is not dangerous to do so, as long as the messages are scriptural and anointed--as I have said, they may really be a blessing. But it is also good to sleep in silence (even with earplugs if necessary), stilling all the senses so that we may commune with our own hearts and receive light therefrom, (Psalms 4:4; 16:7).

Keep in mind here, though, that this is only another natural factor involved in the dream mechanism. Any time that the Spirit of God begins to involve Himself in a given dream (which is possible in a great variety of ways, as we shall see) all of the natural factors begin to become less important, depending upon the degree of God's presence. There are greater and lesser degrees of God's presence in dreams as well as in our waking life.

In natural, unspiritual dreams the thoughts perceived by the mind can be extremely exaggerated or misconstrued-- and that usually in a negative way. However, a spiritually- minded person can use more wisdom, through the Holy Spirit, to interpret information realistically. Mankind has more control over how we entertain thoughts in dreams than we realize--especially when we have the Spirit of God with us.

Also contributory to the quality and content of one's dream experience is the factor of clean air. Since the brain is the physical house of the mind (and the mind is where dreams occur), the brain requires a healthy supply of oxygen in order to function in a healthy way. Fresh air in the room before bedtime helps the brain and the mind (and the dream-thoughts they may entertain) to function in a normal way.

Another interesting fact is that the emotions directly affect the breathing rate, whether we're awake or asleep. If a person goes to sleep while tense, upset, worried, or afraid for some reason, his breathing rate is affected (howsoever minimally or subtly).

Conversely, the breathing rate directly affects the emotions, whether we're awake or asleep. So we can take the initiative and learn to breathe calmly as we meditate on the Lord and cast all our cares upon Him before bedtime. Worshipping the Lord, particularly with the spirit (in other tongues), is ideal at this time because the respiration and emotions will then be in harmony. Meditating on the Lord has the greater influence on our dreams, but breathing peacefully allows oxygen into the brain at a healthy rate--again affecting the dreams in consequence.

Eating before going to sleep generally will affect dreams too. Food qualities, which immediately go into the blood when eaten, are not immediately consumed and therefore continue to enter the brain for awhile. With the brain being thus fed and energized, the thought processes are also stimulated and can prompt dreams. In addition, digestive, nervous, and other body systems are active in the digestion of food, again placing demands upon the carnal mind. Full consumption of food qualities in the blood requires considerably more time, but basic digestion of the main influx of food elements requires about two or three hours, determined mostly by the size of the meal.

There are some foods, drinks, and chemicals which have a direct tendency to keep us awake: such as meats, sweets, coffee, soda, and more. Others help people to sleep: such as hot chocolate, tea, milk, a nightcap, sleeping pills, and other sedatives. It's good to know a little bit about what we're consuming. It's also important to allow Jesus to direct us each night in our before-bedtime snacks and habits. Many people have formed bad habits in this area, Christians and non-Christians alike. But thank God, in Him there is forgiveness and deliverance from every kind of yoke of bondage.

If a person doesn't eat or drink anything at all for a few hours before bedtime (except perhaps water) his digestive system--and his body as a whole--can more easily enter into restful sleep. The mind can therefore entertain more spiritual thoughts for not being summoned by the flesh. Certainly the longer one abstains from eating the more yielded he becomes to spiritual things. (In a fast, a person's flesh is subject to his spirit.)

In the Bible, we see many of God's servants who received visions of the Lord while fasting. The bean (pulse) diet doubtless helped the Prophet Daniel and his fellow Hebrews to receive spiritual and intellectual capacity for wisdom and understanding, (Daniel 1). A yet stricter diet later helped Daniel to receive yet greater revelations of the Lord--namely, that of the extra-natural, (Daniel 10).

Throughout man's history, fasting has often been associated with spiritual visions and revelations. It is universally understood that the flesh body can more easily become disciplined in a fast and the spirit can more easily have ascendency. The Prophet Ezekiel was one of the most disciplined men in the entire Bible. He kept a very strict diet. He was also extremely used of God in visions.

Today too, people who fast make their minds more conducive to spiritual thoughts, visions, and dreams. This applies not only to those who fast, but also to those who keep natural or vegetarian-type diets. Somehow, keeping one's diet natural and simple, as we were originally created to have, helps one's spirit incline to the spiritual realm, as we were created to be.

That's why when people join cults and false religions, particularly those of eastern origin, they usually adopt vegetarianism or a similar diet form. That's also why when Christians want to hear from God and consecrate themselves to Him, they fast or eat simple natural foods, if only for a season.

This is an important point, but it should not obligate us

to fast. When and how we as individuals fast should be completely directed by Jesus. But let us realize here that one result of at least partial abstinence from eating is that "our light will break forth as the morning and rise in obscurity, our darkness will be as the noonday, and the Lord shall guide us," (Isaiah 58:6-11, paraphrased).

Dreams are largely characterized by obscurity and darkness. But as we fast unto the Lord, our Light, Jesus, will rise up and break forth in the midst of our obscure, dark dreams. He stills the stormy sea of confused, threatening thoughts in dreams, and shows us the light so that we can see where He is guiding us.

Partial abstinence, such as for only half a day, may suffice to help us receive God's instruction in a vision of the night, particularly if we're petitioning the Lord on a specific matter. As we have seen, it is often in a dream that God tells us, "This is the way, walk ye in it," (Isaiah 30:21).

4) There are Different Levels of Sleep

Throughout the Bible, there are several Hebrew and Greek words which are translated as "sleep." Each has exclusive characteristics in definition, yet all of them can allow for dreams to occur--especially, of course, when they are supernaturally incited. Obviously, the only exception is when "sleep" refers either to literal death or to figurative death, (as in 1Corinthians 11:30 and Ephesians 5:14, respectively).

According to *Webster's Dictionary, sleep* is "a natural, regularly recurring condition of rest for the body and mind, during which there is little or no conscious thought, sensation, or movement." This most simple and broad definition is enlarged upon by the Bible in the following ways:

Light rest:

Genesis 28:11 And he lighted upon a certain place, and tarried there all that night, because the sun was set; and he took of the stones of that place, and put them for his pillows, and lay down in that place to sleep.

Here the Patriarch Jacob has a lot on his mind. He is also cold, tired, alone, and afraid. He laid down to sleep a *light sleep* (according to the Hebrew rendering), and dreamed a supernatural dream from the Lord. He was strengthened by it and awoke from his sleep and praised God.

Regular physical sleep:

Song of Solomon 5:2a I sleep, but my heart waketh.

This kind of sleep is the most normal and common level. When the average person mentions sleep, this *regular physical sleep* is what he tends to be describing. Even in this natural level of sleep, the heart is awake and may receive natural dreams or dreams from the Lord.

Deep sleep:

Daniel 10:9b Then was I in a deep sleep on my face.

The two Hebrew words for "deep sleep" are *tardemah* and *radam*. Each is used for both *natural deep sleep* and *supernatural deep sleep*. Most often a deep sleep in the Bible was caused by the Lord, and was for a specific reason: either to confound His enemies (as in 1Samuel 26:12, and in Matthew 28:4), or to reveal a profound vision, (as in Genesis 15:12). A *deep sleep from the Lord* (as distinguished from a *natural deep sleep*) and a *trance* are basically the same thing.

Trance:

Acts 11:5a In a trance I saw a vision.

The *trance,* supernatural ecstasy of one or another sort, is an altered state during which the body becomes more or less "stunned" by an "electrical presence" from God. God uses this experience to communicate to the soul in different ways and for different purposes. Most often, a trance in the Bible was experienced outside of the sleeping state, such as when Peter was *praying* on the housetop (Acts 10:9-16), and as when Paul *prayed* in the temple, (Acts 22:17-21). But a trance occasionally occurred during sleep too, (as in Job 4:12-16). This is seen in the Hebrew definitions of *deep sleep from the Lord* and in the contexts in which this term is used. Personally, I too have experienced trances--while awake in prayer, and also while asleep.

Concerning the Human Spirit

Important to our study is an understanding of the triunity of man. God created man in His own image (Genesis 1:27), and God the Father, Son, and Holy Spirit, are spirit, body, and mind, respectively:

John 4:24   God is a Spirit.

Colossians 2:9 (niv)   For in Christ all the fullness of the Deity lives in bodily form.

1Corinthians 2:16b   But we have the mind of Christ.

Our Heavenly Father, God, is a Spirit, and He is also the Father of spirits, (Hebrews 12:9). Jesus Christ is the Son of God Who was manifested in the flesh in order to fulfill His divine mission on earth, (1Timothy 3:16). The mind of Christ is the Holy Spirit Who teaches us all things and illuminates our understanding to God's Word, His will for us, (John 14:26).

Created in the image of God, man also is spirit, mind, and body:

1Thessalonians 5:23 And the very God of peace sanctify you wholly; and I pray God your whole spirit and soul and body be preserved blameless unto the coming of our Lord Jesus Christ.

The spirit of man is the real man on the inside--the person we truly are. The mind (or soul) is the center of the will, emotions, and intellect. The physical body of man is the temple of the true man, a sort of earth suit we need in order to operate in this natural world.

In the beginning of mankind, Adam, the very first man, was in complete union with God. (Incidentally, he too had to be brought into a deep sleep from the Lord before the woman was formed from his side.) When sin entered, all mankind was separated from God *in the spirit*. Man no longer remained the children of God--we became sinners, (Ephesians 2:1-3).

Through Jesus Christ's sacrificial death, burial, and resurrection, we are reconciled unto God in the spirit. Through repentance, by faith, we are cleansed and forgiven of sin, saved from wrath, and recreated into the image of Christ, (Romans 3:23-26; 2Corinthians 5:17-18). This is called being saved, being born-again, and being a Christian, (John 3:3).

If a person is not born-again, God can still speak to him through dreams and otherwise, but *unto* his spirit--not *through* his spirit. The unsaved person's spirit, as opposed to a Christian's, is distant from God, so His dealings with him are more external. When God does talk to an unconverted sinner, the message is usually intended to convict him of his need for Jesus as his Saviour. To this end, the Holy Spirit might remind him of God's Word which he has heard or read. He might show him blessings ahead in his life for obeying the Lord, or dangers ahead for his disobedience. Or He might communicate other messages. But most of the time God's message to a sinner (a non-Christian) will be for him to come to Jesus and "get saved."

Interestingly though, God has been known to speak to

the unsaved, messages applying to other people. It is not uncommon to hear a sinner declare a direction or a warning from God to a friend. Whether or not he realizes it is such is irrelevant. "I've got *a feeling* you shouldn't go there"; "I had a horrible *dream* about what you're planning"; "*Something* tells me that you can trust that person you just met"; and other such like declarations by the unconverted--to Christians or non-Christians--are not at all uncommon. This is one reason why they continue to live without God in their lives--because they are not entirely without His mercy. But again, His messages to sinners are not *through* their spirits (as with Christians) but *unto* them.

When a person is born-again, God's Spirit indwells him. He then has the nature of Christ in him and strong desires toward the Lord. God's fellowship with him is therefore in his spirit, and He communicates to his mind therefrom.

This is why Christians must have their minds renewed to the Word of God and walk by the Spirit of God. The mind of Christ (the will of God, His leadings, and His messages) proceed from His Spirit through our spirits and must be received well in our minds. When we are spiritually-minded (our minds are in harmony with our spirits through the Word of God), God's messages are easy to perceive. His revelations are then clear to us--be they through the inner witness or impressions of the Spirit, or be they through visions and dreams.

Chapter 2

Be Renewed in the Spirit of Your Dream Life

Ephesians 4:23 Be renewed in the spirit of your mind.

Ephesians 4:23-24   And be renewed in the spirit of your mind; And that ye put on the new man, which after God is created in righteousness and true holiness.

We have seen in Chapter 1 that the mind is still awake as we rest in sleep. We have seen that what one learns or perceives during the day forms the major factor which causes or otherwise influences his dreams. We have also seen that as our present life (and how we use it) is indicative of our eternal reward, so our dreams can be indicative of our natural lives. Dreams can show us where we are in light of God's will and how we can move more perfectly therein.

To this end, we should learn to make our thinking new to the Word of God and to the truths about the workings of dreams. When we do this, our minds will be more conducive to God's wisdom in dreams. The renewing of the mind is an ongoing process of maturity, so we'll always have more to learn, more to change, and more to experience in dreams. With the mind in a continuing state of renewing and growth, the entire life is benefitted—during the day and during the night.

I believe that people receive spiritual insights in dreams more often than they realize, but they are easily missed or mishandled because of a lack of knowledge. We know that God speaks to all of us during the day, but unless He speaks by supernatural means, we are to diligently seek His voice with knowledge. Well, since our dream experiences largely depend on and are influenced by our knowledge, we can find the Lord's voice in our dreams when we diligently—with knowledge about dream functions—seek Him there. It has been said, "Ignorance is the curse of God, knowledge is the wing wherewith we fly to Heaven."

When the mind of Christ is formed in us, the details in our dreams are discreetly chosen by our spirits to help us clarify situations and better understand circumstances in our lives. The dreams may include recollections of events, thoughts, and perceptions of experiences of the preceding day, or of the recent or distant past, or a combination of these. The night season can be a time during which the spirit helps the mind to put things in perspective according to the will of God. Our daily thoughts or ideas may be reviewed in dreams in the same way we saw them during the day--only now as seen through the eyes of Jesus.

People we meet, places we go, thoughts we entertain, or any other kind of activity acknowledged by our minds, can be repeated in our night visions--only then in a revised version of the Holy Ghost. In dreams, God often shows us the truth behind what we've perceived the preceding day-- truth we may have been too naturally-minded to see then.

It is man's spirit which speaks to his mind in basic dreams. The Holy Spirit in a Christian often keeps a "low profile" allowing him to call forth God's counsel in his dreams. If it was always God's Spirit directly inspiring our dreams, His messages would always be supernatural and powerful, and we would never have to study to hear from Him.

But is is *we* who must study, *we* who must pray, and *we* who must be strong in the Lord and in the power of His might, (Ephesians 6:10). When our daily devotions and disciplines are observed faithfully, we are then most conducive to the stuff of the supernatural. Only then (outside of a supernatural experience) can we know all things, judge all things, search all things, even the deep things of God. Only then can we enjoy God's life and peace--when we're spiritually-minded.

Romans 8:5-8 For they that are after the flesh do mind the things of the flesh; but they that are after the Spirit the things of the Spirit. For to be carnally minded is death; but to be spiritually minded is life and peace. Because the carnal mind is enmity against God: for it is not subject to the law of God, neither indeed can be. So then they that are in the flesh cannot please God.

Being carnally minded means leaning onto our own understanding. Natural wisdom, knowledge, and understanding are not in subjection to God. The natural mind is in rebellion and cannot please Him. We must lean onto the Holy Spirit as we gain knowledge and He will give us a living understanding of His will.

Often we've learned philosophies of life--wisdoms of this lower world--which have benefitted us in our various undertakings, and we find it hard to learn new principles, new ways of thinking. There's a certain amount of truth to the old maxim "You can't teach an old dog new tricks." But the fact remains, "I can do all things through Christ which strengtheneth me," (Philippians 4:13).

God can take a demon-possessed man and transform him into an Evangelist, such as the Gadarene demoniac, (Mark 5:1-20). God can take an adulteress and transform her into a precious testimony for the Lord, such as the Samaritan woman at Jacob's well, (John 4:5-42). God can take a man who persecutes Christians and transform him into an apostle of Jesus Christ, such as Saul of Tarsus, (Acts 9:1-22). God can take an erroneous, carnal way of thinking and transform it into the mind of Christ:

Romans 12:2   And be not conformed to this world: but be ye transformed by the renewing of your mind, that ye may prove what is that good, and acceptable, and perfect, will of God.

The word "transformed" here (Greek: *metamorphoo*) indicates "a complete change." From this word we get our English word "metamorphosis," which means "a total newness of form, structure, and function, which occurs rather suddenly." It doesn't mean a growing as from a kitten to a cat, or as from a puppy to a dog. It means a total change as from a tadpole to a frog, or as from a caterpillar to a butterfly, or from a sinner to a saint, or from a carnal mind to a spiritual mind.

Jesus Christ, the living Word of God, gave Himself for us so that we can be *transformed,* recreated into His likeness. That's why we can *imitate* Him (according to the Greek rendering of Ephesians 5:1). We can see Jesus in the mirror of His Word and be "changed" (again *metamorphoo*) into the same image from glory to glory to glory, even as by the Spirit of the Lord, (2Corinthians 3:18).

In the "new birth" experience our spirits are automatically changed, transformed into the image of Christ-- all things in us are new, all things in us are now of God, (2Corinthians 5:17-18). But our minds are still subject to this natural world where time exists. Therefore, we must work out into the natural realm, in the process of time, the salvation we have received in our spirits.

This is a gradual process of decreasing or crucifying the fleshly mind so that the willing spirit may come forth and lift up Christ. Only when Christ is lifted up and magnified through us can men be drawn unto Him, (John 12:32). To this end, the written Word of God illuminates the eyes of our understanding by the Spirit of the Lord.

As we are gradually renewed and conformed to God's Word, we become more and more glorious, holy still, and presentable to the Lord. This speaks not only of our spirits and minds, but also of our bodies which are His temple:

Hebrews 10:21-22 And having an High Priest over the house of God; Let us draw near with a true heart in full assurance of faith, having our hearts sprinkled from an evil conscience, and our bodies washed with pure water.

Ephesians 5:25-27 Husbands, love your wives, even as Christ also loved the Church, and gave Himself for it; That He might sanctify and cleanse it with the washing of water by the Word, That He might present it to Himself a glorious Church, not having spot, or wrinkle, or any such thing; but that it should be holy and without blemish.

God's Word will straighten out and remove every spot, wrinkle, blemish, and any such thing from your life. Then He will fill you with His glory, His manifested presence, and you begin to have measures of faith you didn't have before: faith to love other people, faith to give and pray for others, faith to be a blessing in general, and faith to go to sleep in peace knowing that the Lord will visit you during the night to review your day with you, and show you things you must know for tomorrow. With your mind renewed to the Word of God, you'll be able to prove, to show, to demonstrate for yourself, what is the will of God for you. Remember, *you* must renew your mind so that *you* will prove God's will in your life.

2Timothy 2:20-21 But in a great house there are not only vessels of gold and of silver, but also of wood and of earth; and some to honour, and some to dishonour. If a man therefore purge himself from these, he shall be a vessel unto honour, sanctified, and meet for the Master's use, and prepared unto every good work.

The Body of Christ is here likened unto a great house, and each individual Christian is likened unto a vessel--either an honourable one, or a dishonourable one. Each one must purge himself of his own dishonourable stuff of "wood and earth" (sins), and adorn himself with God's honourable "gold, silver, and precious stones" (holiness, righteousness, obedience, and preparedness in the things of God).

God purges and sanctifies us by His own power, but we are to cooperate with Him by an act of our own free wills, (Isaiah 1:19). This is the way by which we become fit for the Master's use and prepared unto every good work. And this is also the way by which we are to become prepared unto every good dream. Any dream through which the Lord might speak to us will most easily manifest when it's built upon the sure foundation of Jesus Christ.

Hebrews 12:14 Follow... holiness, without which no man shall see the Lord.

Without a holy, consecrated, and renewed mind, one will

not easily see the Lord's messages in dreams.

In the Old Testament, the Levitical priests had to sanctify themselves before entering the Holy Place of the Tabernacle--and more particularly the Holy of Holies. Before covenanting with God at Mount Sinai, the children of Israel had to sanctify themselves for three days in order to endure the revelation of the presence of God. In the New Testament, Mary, the virgin mother of Jesus, had been living a consecrated life unto the Lord. No wonder she was highly favoured of God and was chosen to conceive Jesus by the Holy Spirit. Gabriel himself, the angel which stands in the very presence of God, visited and communicated personally to Mary the divine plan of God.

The disciples in the Upper Room had been repenting, fasting, praying, and studying God's Word, to show themselves approved unto God. Well, they were approved. They'd been sanctifying themselves unto the Lord and expecting from Him a supernatural visitation and were therefore able to receive the mighty enduement of power from on high! They didn't draw back when the Holy Ghost fell on the Day of Pentecost. Likewise we, if sanctified and fit for the Master's use, will incline (and not decline) to receive revelations from Him.

King David, while trying to decide where the Ark (symbolic of God's presence) should rest, that is, where the Temple should be built, made this vow unto God:

Psalms 132:3-5   Surely I will not come into the tabernacle of my house, nor go up into my bed; I will not give sleep to mine eyes, or slumber to mine eyelids, Until I find out a place for the Lord, an habitation for the mighty God of Jacob.

Similarly, the Body of Christ may pray, "I will not go to sleep until I find a place, a secret place for the Lord in my heart and in my mind, wherein I shall find peace and not be afraid."

As we edify for the Lord a dwelling-place in our souls before sleeptime, He can more easily visit us in the night seasons and instruct us. The Lord is pleased to dwell in the places we set apart for Him. Let's become worthy vessels of God--gold, silver, and precious stones. Only then can the precious things of God be added unto us. Jesus said that unto everyone that has shall more be given (Matthew 25:29), and that precious pearls are not to be given to swine, (Matthew 7:6).

Again I emphasize that the sovereign God can communicate to anyone and at any time, regardless of one's preparation in the Word or lack of it. But here we are concerned with the role *we* have in studying, living in holiness, seeking Him by night on the bed, and otherwise preparing the way for the Lord's counsel in dreams.

Renewing the mind is a gradual process which involves reading the Word of God, praying, fellowshipping with the Lord, fellowshipping with other Christians, and being involved with the works of the Holy Spirit generally--all on a regular basis. It is necessary to feed and influence the mind's thought processes with everything involving God, and then to live in harmony with Him, in order to establish His Word in our lives.

Sometimes people simply want a "how to" method of receiving blessings from God, even to the neglect of regular devotions. I do not want to minimize the attention owed to biblical principles of receiving and how to enforce them. This study itself is largely concerned with such principles. But emphasis must be placed on our more normal Christian duties: reading the Bible, praying, going to Church, and living purely before the Lord in general. Hereby we more fully and soundly make our lives conducive to God's blessings and visitations.

We often think God's glory, His presence, is exclusively celestial, reserved for the "Higher world." But the Bible says that the *whole earth* is full of His glory (Psalms 72:19), that He has created *all things* for His pleasure (Revelation 4:11), and that it is *through His servants* that His will is wrought *in the earth* as it is in Heaven, (Matthew 6:10).

By this we know, and by faith see, that in natural things also is the glory of God revealed--not only in the sight of the Lord, but also in the sight of men; and not only in supernatural experiences such as visions and dreams, but also in basic, regular exercises of worship. Divine providence in this natural, lower world where we live often reveals the glory of God in more undeniable ways than anything else.

A person may be asking the Lord if he is in His perfect will. This is good, but he might be expecting God to confirm or reveal His will supernaturally--through a personal prophecy, vision, or dream. The person might even be using some principles which can help him to hear from God, some of which are shared in this book. This too is good.

But God might be pleased to answer the person through natural situations and circumstances. This is particularly true if he has prepared the way of the Lord in his life by observing his basic Christian duties. God involves Himself in the affairs of men and communicates to us by what is provided naturally. Providence is the wheel or course of life's natural events (James 3:6), and herein we're to acknowledge and praise Him as well as in divine communications.

We have heard the popular maxim, "No news is good news." Well, it may be that "No dreams indicates good dreams." Or rather, dreams not being recalled may indicate that all is well, you're in the will of God, or you've got enough to go on so far. While sleeping, we are dreaming most of the time even if we don't remember the dreams. And our daily circumstances often speak more loudly of God's work in our lives than do our dreams.

God does speak to men in dreams sometimes because they don't listen to Him when they're awake, (Job 33:14-16). But if we are obeying Him with all that is within us, He may not need to open our ears while we're in slumberings upon the bed. We can pray that we will remember the dreams that we do have, but we should be at peace believing God is pleased with us if we don't receive specific insights in dreams inspired of Him. The fact that we would like to hear from Him is itself a good indication that our hearts are already yielded to His will, especially if we're willing to receive correction, if necessary, as well as blessing. Dreams (or any other form of communication from God) often disclose negative attributes needing to be dealt with, as well as positive ones worthy of praise.

As far as concerns using biblical principles, let's consider the important factor of confessing (speaking) God's Word by faith. This means choosing certain Scripture verses and quoting them for yourself personally--calling them yours, speaking them so that they will become alive and operative in your life specifically.

Romans 4:17 (amp) As it is written, I have made you the father of many nations.--He was appointed our father--in the sight of God in Whom he believed, Who gives life to the dead and speaks of the nonexistent things that [He has foretold and promised] as if they [already] existed.

The King James Version says, "God... calleth those things which be not as though they were."

God calls things into existence by declaring that they exist even before they actually do! When God told His covenant man Abraham, "I have made you the father of many nations," Abraham had only one child, Ishmael, lamentably from his wife's maid. There was no hope of having children by his wife Sarai because she was very old and physically unable to conceive. However, God continually confessed His Word to change this situation.

The name "Abraham" means "father of a multitude." God changed it from "Abram" when He promised him many descendants. Each time someone addressed Abraham they confessed God's will over him--that is, God's "Word," (Greek: *rhema,* "a flowing, pouring word; a spontaneous utterance of the Spirit").

Each time Abraham heard his name, it strengthened his faith in God's will because faith comes by hearing God's *specific word,* His *rhema* for us, (Romans 10:17). The name "Sarah," which God changed from "Sarai," means "mother of nations," so she also was strengthened in faith each time she heard her name.

Unceasingly God's will was thereby being spoken until it came to pass. This same Word of God also continued to be spoken prophetically by God's prophets down through the centuries. Each time Christ's birth was prophesied in the Old Testament, God's promise was being spoken into the earth--for Christ is the Seed of Abraham in Whom the nations are justified by faith.

This Word, God's covenant with Abraham, began to come to pass when his son Isaac was born, and continued to be fulfilled through his lineage. In the New Testament, this Word was made flesh and dwelt among us in the form of Jesus Christ. Since then, this same Word is yet being fulfilled each time a person is born-again. When we become Christ's, we become Abraham's Seed (Galatians 3:29), for he is the father of the faithful.

God is alive and full of power. He properly channels His power by using words. The specific words He uses directly decree and enforce what those words name. When He wants the dead to live, His Spirit speaks, "Live!" When He wants the lame to walk, His Spirit speaks, "Walk!" When He wants the blind to see, His Spirit says, "See!"

Our responsibility is to learn through prayer what God's Spirit is saying at a given time, and agree with Him. As Christians, we are God's voice in the earth, and as we hear the words of His Spirit in us we are to vocalize those words. These are the words which we are to confess and decree in the earth, and because they are inspired of Him, they have a prophetic element and will come to pass.

As we have seen with God's covenant with Abraham, we should speak the desired end before it exists--until it is manifested. Needful to understand here is that the desired end can be directly inspired by the Spirit of God, or it can be simply permitted by Him. In other words, there are greater and lesser degrees of inspiration from God. At times, God's Spirit may directly inspire us to speak specific words of healing (for ourselves or for someone else), and they will come to pass. At other times, He may simply permit such words to be spoken, and they will come to pass. His words are available to us, directly and indirectly, but we must at least sense the liberty to speak what we would in prayer, otherwise we are not to speak.

When it comes to certain kinds of words, prayers, prophecies, or confessions of faith, we must not utter them unless we are specifically, directly inspired by the Spirit of God. Very unspecific kinds of prayers, general blessings, we are more free to speak. For me to pray, prophesy, or confess over you that you will be a missionary to Africa, or that you will pastor a particular Church, or something else of great magnitude, I must be directly instructed by God. However, I'm more free to pray, prophesy, or confess over you that you will serve the Lord *generally,* or that *if it's God's will* He'll provide a spouse for you, or something else according to God's *basic* will for everyone.

In this latter type of prayer, God is allowed great liberty to use my words as He desires--so He can use this prayer. If I declare specific decrees in prayer without His leading, I can ruin someone's life (including my own) because a Christian's words have much power. Then God will have to turn down the power volume in my prayers until He can trust me more fully.

Ordinarily, while we begin praying or confessing God's general word for a given situation, He will gradually begin inspiring certain words. He will begin to change the space of liberty in which we are moving in a given prayer-- either to pull us out of certain words, or to pull us into certain words. He thus leads us into the areas He wants us to address in prayer. And the more He leads us with specific words in prayer, the more effective they will be, and less strength will be required of us because His Spirit is then flowing freely.

Specifically inspired words in prayer are as a sharpened iron ax, and general, uninspired ones are less sharp and require more strength, more faith, (Ecclesiastes 10:9-10). As we pray by faith, we should seek the leading of the Holy Spirit, again by faith. But if He doesn't lead us specifically, we're doing alright where we are.

To call forth God's counsel in our spirits, we have great liberty at all times to decree the following basic truths:

1Corinthians 1:30 But of Him are ye in Christ Jesus, Who of God is made unto us wisdom, and righteousness, and sanctification, and redemption.

1Corinthians 2:16 For who hath known the mind of the Lord, that he may instruct Him? But we have the mind of Christ.

John 14:26 But the Comforter, which is the Holy Ghost, whom the Father will send in My Name, He shall teach you all things, and bring all things to your remembrance, whatsoever I have said unto you.

John 16:13 Howbeit when He, the Spirit of Truth, is come, He will guide you into all truth: for He shall not speak of Himself; but whatsoever He shall hear, that shall He speak: and He will shew you things to come.

1John 2:20 But ye have an unction from the Holy One, and ye know all things.

In accordance with these preceding Scriptures, we may pray thus:

"Jesus Christ is made unto me wisdom. I have God's wisdom, the mind of Christ, in me. I know all things (as they become needful to know) because I have an unction, an anointing from the Holy One. The Holy Spirit comforts me, teaches me all things, guides me into all truth, shows me things to come, and reminds me of Jesus' words."

This prayer, and other such like "confessions of faith,"

may be spoken and decreed over yourself often and at any time because they are fundamental and always apply to us as Christians. A good time to pray this way is before going to sleep because you hereby prepare your soul for the counsel of the Holy Spirit during sleep.

The following verses can likewise be prayed, and they apply more directly to our sleep:

Proverbs 3:24 When thou liest down, thou shalt not be afraid: yea, thou shalt lie down, and thy sleep shall be sweet.

Proverbs 6:22 When thou goest, it shall lead thee; when thou sleepest, it shall keep thee; and when thou awakest, it shall talk with thee.

Psalms 4:8 I will both lay me down in peace, and sleep: for Thou, Lord, only makest me dwell in safety.

Joshua 1:8 This book of the law shall not depart out of thy mouth; but thou shalt meditate therein day and night, that thou mayest observe to do according to all that is written therein: for then thou shalt make thy way prosperous, and then thou shalt have good success.

Micah 2:1 Woe to them that devise iniquity, and work evil upon their beds! when the morning is light, they practise it, because it is in the power of their hand.

Inverting this last verse, we can say, "Blessing to them that devise good, and work good plans upon their beds! When the morning is light, they practise it, because it is in the power of their hand."

In accordance with these preceding Scriptures, we may pray thus:

"I meditate (speak, ponder) God's Word in my life, day and night. I observe, according to all that is written therein, how to prosper and succeed. I lie down and my sleep is sweet because God's Word keeps me; I am not afraid. I devise good plans upon my bed. When I awaken,

God's Word leads and talks with me concerning my ideas, and I can practise them because they're in the power of my hand. All to the glory of God in Jesus' Name."

Other helpful Bible selections for prayers of confession include: the whole armour of God, the ministry of angels, the Name of Jesus, and the Blood of Jesus. By thus renewing our mind and our dream life to the Word of God, we arm ourselves against evil spirits who might attempt to attack us in the night seasons. We may confidently confess, or pray, whatever we know about our God-given powers. Obviously, we cannot pray and believe God for what we don't know, and so many Christians suffer unnecessarily:

Hosea 4:6a   My people are destroyed for lack of knowledge.

As we are faithful, diligent, and bold to renew our minds to the Word of God, we will be strong to resist the adversary and no day or night weapon of his can prosper against us, (Isaiah 54:17a). Satan not only attacks but also has been known to transform himself into an "angel of light" to deceive, (2Corinthians 11:14). However, as armed soldiers, we will not be ignorant of His day or night devices, but will be sharp to perceive and defeat them before they even manifest, (2Corinthians 2:11).

We may pray:

"Lord God, I thank You for equipping me with Your mighty armour--which no demon can penetrate. You have given me authority over all of the enemy's violent forces, and nothing shall by any means hurt me, (Luke 10:19). Your precious Blood helps me overcome Satan and any of his cohorts. Your Name is my strong tower in which I trust. Your light dispels all darkness. Your angels protect me and minister for me as I rest in Your presence. Lord, only You may visit me in the night and seal instructions in me as I sleep. In Jesus' Name. Amen."

If you feel you should, on a given night, you might specifically address Satan before retiring:

"I command you wicked spirits to be bound. You will not assault me or in any way influence or communicate to me. The power of God is with me, and I resist you, Satan. In Jesus' Name!"

Personally, I address Satan in prayers of spiritual warfare to resist him only when I perceive his presence in any degree, or when God specifically instructs me to. We may speak against evil forces to bind them by faith, but often they are automatically bound through our general prayers. Either way, before sleeping we should be satisfied in our spirits that no demon or weapon formed against us shall prosper as we sleep. Sensitivity and unafraidness to spiritual things is important in these matters.

One night after much prayer, I was getting ready to go to sleep, and the thought came, "Before sleeping, resist the forces of darkness." Then I thought, "That's just a thought, that's not really the Lord talking to me. I've already prayed, I'm already in the Spirit. I'll be alright."

So I went to sleep.

That night the Lord gave me a supernatural experience in which I left my body, flew in the spiritual realm with an angel, and heard the voice of Jesus. Upon descending and gradually reentering my body, I perceived a demonic spirit bothering my left ear and distracting me from hearing Jesus' last words to me. I asked Jesus, "Why don't You do something about him? Don't You protect us supernaturally from evil spirits when You incite a supernatural experience?

But He didn't answer my questions.

Gradually I descended back into my body. I turned to the demon and rebuked him in Jesus' Name. And he left.

While reviewing each part of the experience, I again asked Jesus why He didn't do something about that demon, for it was because of him that I missed the last part of what He had told me. Jesus then brought to my remembrance the fact that He had warned me in that thought before sleeping to resist the forces of darkness.

Then I understood that He equips us for what's to come

so that we will always have the victory. But if we don't take heed to His instructions, it may cost us. I also understood that God speaks in our thoughts. However, if He doesn't warn us of an approaching enemy, He will deal with him personally, especially in supernatural experiences.

Again, when praying certain Scriptures before bedtime, we can be as specific as our petitions require. If you are seeking healing from God, you should pray the Scriptures which promise you divine healing, particularly if they name your condition, (such as Psalms 146:8).

Basically, we are free to pray God's general will for us as we like and can also paraphrase the Bible, make up our own Scripture-based forms, and even make heartfelt repetitions. Jesus said that the prayers of the heathen are vain repetitions, (Matthew 6:7). But as true Christians, our prayers are from the heart, and we can repeat them as often as we desire.

Now one prayer which many children are taught to repeat before bedtime is this:

> "Now I lay me down to sleep.
> I pray the Lord my soul to keep.
> If I should die before I wake,
> I pray the Lord my soul to take."

It's nice, it's sweet, but it's too "death-minded." Surely we should understand that if we were to die while sleeping we would go to be in the presence of the Lord in Paradise, if we are a true Christian, (2Corinthians 5:8). But to recite this prayer every night might make us think that it's very possible that we will die in our sleep, and that we have no control over our sleep experiences. Perhaps we should prefer this improved version:

> "Now I lay me down to sleep.
> I know the Lord my soul does keep.
> I shall be blessed before I wake,
> For in the Lord I meditate."

My dear nephew, Chris Diaz, testified to me that he prayed this rendition one night when he was under nine years of age:

"Now I lay me down to sleep.
I pray the Lord my soul to keep.
If I should die before I wake,
I pray the Lord my soul to take.
And I cover my mother, my father,
My brother, and myself,
And the rest of my family,
And all of my friends,
With the Blood of Jesus,
With the Blood of Jesus. Amen."

He clearly stated that he repeated "With the Blood of Jesus" by direct inspiration of the Lord. Jesus Himself taught him to claim "The Blood of Jesus" over himself before bedtime. And this is something we should all do, always.

With children, bedtime stories can be instrumental in starting their dreams off on the right track. We should prefer Bible stories and our own godly originals. If we use non-Christian literature, it should be prayerfully chosen and explained with God's wisdom. We should cautiously screen all children's books to make sure that humanistic or otherwise ungodly ideas aren't slyly sown in their minds during their formative years. And after reading to our children we can pray for them.

If we allow our children to sleep with dolls, teddy bears, puppets, toy soldiers, and similar playthings, they should be of the most modest sorts. They may even represent figures from the Bible. Representative figures or toys connected to spiritual powers shown on secular television programs should be clearly forbidden--with an explanation, if appropriate. Any figures or toys we do allow should be prayed over when bought.

Now a lot of times, after praying in any of the ways shown above, we still know not how to pray as we ought. We have prayed some Scriptures, we have bound Satan, we have welcomed and worshipped the Lord, we have acknowledged the angelic ministries on our behalf, and we have armed ourselves with the weapons of our warfare.

But, good as all these kinds of prayers really are, they may not always be enough. Often certain utterances released through our spirits hold the keys which will unlock certain mysteries we desire to solve, and tap the anointings we require. Speaking with other tongues in these matters becomes a vital part of our prayers.

Romans 8:26 Likewise the Spirit also helpeth our infirmities: for we know not what we should pray for as we ought: but the Spirit itself maketh intercession for us with groanings which cannot be uttered.

1Corinthians 14:2 For he that speaketh in an unknown tongue speaketh not unto men, but unto God: for no man understandeth him; howbeit in the spirit he speaketh mysteries.

1Corinthians 14:14 For if I pray in an unknown tongue, my spirit prayeth, but my understanding is unfruitful.

With other tongues, my spirit prays, speaks unto God the mysteries I cannot express with my natural mind. I don't always know how to pray as I should, so the Holy Spirit intercedes for me by taking hold together with my spirit in groanings which cannot be uttered/spoken in articulate speech, in my regular kind of speech. He helps me to offer my petitions worthily unto the Lord.

Once they are in His hands, my prayers will begin to be answered. And if I desire to receive a revelation of God's will in a dream, praying in other tongues before bedtime will edify my spirit and stir up, call forth, the thoughts of the Holy Spirit. Then while I'm sleeping, my mind can more easily receive and interpret the mysteries I seek clarity concerning.

Ideally, we should pray as we are inspired to by the Holy Spirit, or as we may sense the liberty to pray. Additionally, we can pray as shown above--speaking mysteries in the spirit with other tongues--and ask God to honour and work through our prayers. We are co-labourers with Him (1Corinthians 3:9), and we can initiate prayer and, at times, move the hand of God.

Sometimes the Lord moves in a certain way and we are to follow Him. At other times, He's not moving. We can then make a move of some sort, by faith, and He may say, "Okay, we'll go that way."

Life in Jesus Christ is most colorful and interesting. Each day, each night, and each situation necessitates our seeking His leading. In any given situation, we are to seek and follow His leading--or, if we don't see Him, step out by faith in the knowledge and understanding we have in His Word.

If the Lord approves of the way we have chosen, He will support us, back us up. If He disapproves, He will reveal His way for that situation specifically--in other words, He will speak His *rhema,* His "current word which His Spirit has for us at that particular time." But even when He changes our plans, God will still bless us for taking the initiative and walking by faith--as long as we do it without being presumptuous. Our faith in His Word pleases God, (Hebrews 11:6).

We must understand that God has given us all the authority and equipment which we need in order to occupy until He comes. Often we take a back seat spiritually and do nothing to prepare for His visitations. We say, "I don't have to help God. If He wants to talk to me in a dream, there's nothing I can do to help Him. Either way it's up to Him." That might sound humble, but it's erroneous. Jesus said, "Behold, I give power unto *you,*" (Luke 10:19). That means it's up to *us* to do something, if only to prepare the way for Him.

The Bible also says that *we* must study God's Word, *we* must put on the whole armour of God, *we* must renew our minds, *we* must conceive devices on our beds, and it is *our* minds which instruct us in the night seasons. The understanding needful here lies in the fact that we are labourers together with God. The important point is that there are greater and lesser degrees of inspiration from God.

When His presence visits us in a great way, He seeks to fill the lodging we have prepared for Him by His Word in us. If we have not founded for Him a lodging-place, we'll suffer shame for nakedness. That's why He gives us tools to build His kingdom, to prepare the way of the Lord-- first in our hearts and minds, then in our lives and in the world around us.

If His presence is not visiting us in a great, spectacular way, He is yet with us, and *we* can draw out the deep water of counsel in our hearts by using the understanding we have in His Word, (Proverbs 20:5). Simply stated, at times God Himself will spring up and pour out His Spirit upon us, as from a spring or fountain. At other times, we've got to dig deep, by faith, and draw out the water of His Spirit, as from a well.

With this in mind, we see how we can exercise the powers of the Spirit of God in more areas than many Christians have learned hitherto. Some of our consciences have been seared, desensitized by the lies of Satan. By not using the whole armour of God, we have had our guards down, and we have allowed mental and spiritual "giants" to take up residence in our souls over the years. False teachings, unscriptural principles of life, destructive thought patterns, and demonic strongholds, might all be in our minds as the walls of Jericho, (Joshua 6). But if we will obey God as did Joshua, the strongholds will bow and we can take the spoils!

Deep down in the great repository of the subconscious born-again spirit, there are answers to our questions, keys to secret knowledge, dissolving of doubts, solutions to personal and universal problems, and much, much more. That's also where we get the interpretations of tongues, of visions, and of dreams. A true Christian soldier is a warrior on the offensive, taking back the spiritual territory which Satan stole.

If only we would dare to go forth and retrieve this land, we could edify in us an excellent spirit through which Jesus Christ can easily glorify Himself. And in the night seasons our dreams and their interpretations will more fully provide the mind of Christ we require.

Setting the Mind in Gear

As stated earlier, there are many different ways we can pray before bedtime. We can choose certain prayers, or we can pray the specific words which God inspires us to. Additionally, while we're approaching the Lord with our specific petitions and casting all our cares over on Him, we can prepare our minds for desired dreams. The mind may be "set in gear" before sleeping so as to prompt the mind to dream certain dreams.

Remember that if Jesus is not directly inspiring a dream, it doesn't mean He's not in it. If we are trusting fully in His Word and in prayer to receive certain insights in dreams, and He doesn't direct us specifically, He is yet with us, even though indirectly. We need not fear entering the dream realm and experimenting in it when our minds and motives have been completely laid at the feet of Jesus.

Now one might say, "But the Bible says that we are not supposed to listen to our dreams which *we* cause to be dreamed." Actually, in the context of Jeremiah 29:8, God is referring to false prophets. The Jews were captives in Babylon and were to remain so for seventy years, according to God's will. Well, false prophets began to prophesy that the Jews would return to Jerusalem shortly. Because this is what they wanted, they spoke and meditated about this and encouraged themselves to return. This caused the Jews and their false prophets to dream of returning.

Even though their false dreams were never fulfilled, they yet entertained such false dreams. Had they spoken and meditated on God's will, and encouraged themselves in His Word, they would have caused themselves to dream in accordance with God's will--which was for them to remain in Babylon for seventy years.

This is what we must do. Meditate on His Word, His will, and yield our souls unto Him before bedtime, then ask Him to lead our dreams by the way which they should go. Then we will have a Shepherd for our dreams, and know they're blessed of Him. When our dreams are not of God--Jesus is not glorified in them--we will be troubled because there is then no Shepherd, (Zechariah 10:2). Conversely, when Jesus is in our dreams, we will be led as a flock to green pastures, prosperous areas of one kind or another.

I also submit that we are always causing the dreams we have anyway. By allowing ourselves to perceive what we do during the day, we are determining what our minds will continue to meditate on in dreams. The mind is a channel through which ideas are acknowledged and interpreted. Setting the mind in gear simply means steering the mind in the right direction--toward the things of God--so that our dreams will begin on the right track.

Setting the mind in gear means directly meditating on the issues and the Scriptures relating to the situation you want clarity about. Just before going to sleep, review in your mind experiences and thoughts you had during the day. Ask God questions about these and ask Him to give you wisdom, insight, confirmation, and revelations about these through dreams. Again, if He doesn't stop you or lead you elsewhere in your prayer, you have the liberty to pray and to dream about what you have chosen to. After asking God questions, seek the answers by meditating on the Word which applies, for the answers are all in His Word--it's all in the Good Book.

The spirit and the mind never fully sleep, and when the body is beginning to rest in sleep, natural reasonings and attitudes tend to rest also. Faith, which is of the spirit, can then operate more freely because carnal thoughts are not as active to hinder. Faith is needed to receive the revelations and guidance sought.

Faith comes by hearing, and hearing by the Word of God (Romans 10:17), so renew your mind by His Word.

By faith we should awaken our minds for service in the night so that the dream mechanism may fully perform its role. We can please and receive from God only by faith, and faith is most powerfully released when fleshly lusts and proud imaginations are asleep. Faith will make alive and productive in our minds the wisdom we need which has already been stirred up in our spirits.

We must walk by faith, and not by sight, not by our natural understanding, (2Corinthians 5:7). It's going to take a lot of faith on our part to abandon our natural little "boats" and walk on water as did the Apostle Peter, (or better yet, as did Jesus Himself). Had Joshua and the Israelites attempted to spoil Jericho by what they understood naturally, they would never have conquered the Promised Land--wherein abode precious milk and honey in abundance.

We too should learn to trust Jesus to take us by the hand and bring us through to higher spiritual heights and to deeper spiritual depths, because we too have been promised a Precious Land.

How much influence or control can we ultimately gain over our dreams and dreaming? With our minds completely renewed to God's Word, will we eventually be able to cause ourselves to dream as we want, whenever and however we want, or if we want, to not dream at all?

There are three points which help us answer these questions. First of all, dream functions are not independent of the regular waking thought processes. As we saw in Chapter 1, dreams are mostly made up of what we have already acknowledged or perceived in our real life. And since our minds are constantly being renewed--there's always more to learn, we'll never be perfectly flawless and sinless until we're glorified like Jesus--our dream life is being gradually renewed day by day too, (2Corinthians 4:16).

As we grow in the knowledge of the Lord, serving Him with our whole heart, soul, mind, and strength, our dream life will undoubtedly perform its proper functions and serve us well. But as our daily thoughts often divert from

God's thoughts, so do our nightly ones. His ways are higher than our ways, His thoughts are higher than ours, (Isaiah 55:9). We'll always have to keep our minds in check, while we're awake, and while we're asleep.

Secondly, the sleep/dream state is an open arena to the spiritual, supernatural dimensions. It is a very abstract, unpredictable, often unintelligible realm. There are laws by which all activities, natural and spiritual, must abide. But the devil, a spiritual outlaw, rules the darkness of this world, and we contact that darkness in the night seasons. Therefore, our influence over our dream life is limited-- mainly because our minds are not perfect, and also because of the devil's influences.

Finally, God uses dreams to speak to us, and He can reveal Himself when and as He pleases. So He will never allow a man to control his whole mind or his whole dream life independently of Him. The dream state is a great channel which must remain open to communication, unbound and unrestricted, even though there is a lot which we can and should do to supervise and set our minds in gear to dream. Remember, God created dreaming so that He could inspire and seal His instructions in us.

When Jesus says, "Come up hither," He first comes to us where we're at and are able to receive Him, and He offers His hand in a way we can receive it. We're supposed to have faith and put our hand in His and say:

"Yes Jesus, I'll go where You take me, Good Shepherd. Yea, though I walk through a new path unknown to me, a new revelation, a new kind of dream, I will not fear, for You are with me. Your Word comforts and enlightens me, keeps me in sound revelations and ever-increasing light so I be not confused or overcome by darkness. Yes Lord, here am I, send me into that higher height and deeper depth of Your Word by a revelation of Your Holy Spirit. Yes Lord, I incline to dreams and revelations of Thee."

Be they supernatural dreams and revelations, or be they basic wisdoms and messages through dreams, we're to be open to God and to the dreams through which He speaks.

Chapter 3

Sleep in Heavenly Peace

Proverbs 3:24 When thou liest down, thou shalt not
be afraid: yea, thou shalt lie down, and
thy sleep shall be sweet.

Psalms 23 **The Lord is my Shepherd; I shall not want. He maketh me to lie down in green pastures: He leadeth me beside the still waters. He restoreth my soul: He leadeth me in the paths of righteousness for His Name's sake. Yea, though I walk through the valley of the shadow of death, I will fear no evil: for Thou art with me; Thy rod and Thy staff they comfort me. Thou preparest a table before me in the presence of mine enemies: Thou anointest my head with oil; my cup runneth over. Surely goodness and mercy shall follow me all the days of my life: and I will dwell in the house of the Lord for ever.**

With Jesus Christ as our Shepherd, we can lie down to sleep knowing He will lead us in our dreams to prosperous fields (green pastures). In other words, He may be pleased to show us how we are to prosper in a certain area so that we will not lack. He may even give us an idea for a witty invention, perhaps a great one. Remember, dreams are partly meant to be visions which provide us with ideas and goals we are to set.

Countless Christians have received new inventions, ideas for businesses, directions for their lives and ministries, confirmations about whom to marry (or whom not to marry), or whom to associate with (or whom not to associate with), and other insights and revelations from the Lord, in dreams.

The *valley of the shadow of death* may be understood as the spiritual darkness which often seeks to hover over us as we sleep. A valley rests between two lofty places. When our daily thoughts are lofty and proud, our nightly rest may be a *valley experience.*

People who exalt themselves shall be abased, (Matthew 23:12). If they commit evil out of a wicked heart, daily, they may experience unpleasant sleep, nightly. They can't sleep in peace because they have a guilty conscience.

Conversely, those who humbly serve the Lord daily can be edified nightly. People who maintain a pure, loving, Christ-like heart, are able to enjoy sweet sleep with God's blessings every night. They sleep well because they have a clear conscience.

The *shadow of death* (from the Hebrew word *tsalmaveth*) indicates "sinking into darkness, beginning to approach darkness." The darkness can represent calamity or death, and can be literal or spiritual. In sleep, one often begins to approach dark areas such as fears, doubts, torments, bad memories, evil spirits, or even death.

Because the sleeping state is partially spiritual, when one enters sleep without the whole armour of God he is vulnerable to a degree to that darkness. If a person is not a Christian, he is at the mercy of that darkness. There's not much he can do to avoid nightmares and other works of Satan. Personally, I don't understand how a person can survive without Jesus' lordship and power.

If a person is a Christian, the devil would like to hinder him from entering into deep fellowship with the Lord in sleep. This is because a Christian can gain powerful knowledge, insights, and anointings in dreams which can help him to become a victorious Christian, to say the least.

One of Satan's main devices is fear. If he can convince a Christian that he is not safe in those profound spiritual arenas visible in sleep, or that they are unattainable, the Christian will remain inactive and unfruitful in sleep. But if he learns to truly trust Jesus as he walks through the *valley* of the shadow of death, fearing no evil, calling Satan's bluff, he may very possibly see the Lord in dreams. To all who dwell in the *secret place* of the Most High and abide under the *shadow of the Almighty,* God says:

Psalms 91:5 Thou shalt not be afraid for the terror by night.

Jesus also says:

John 14:27 Peace I leave with you, My peace I give unto you: not as the world giveth, give I unto you. Let not your heart be troubled, neither let it be afraid.

We may see Jesus in our dreams in supernatural ways,

or we may see Him in His wisdoms. We can see Jesus in our dreams constantly, in one way or another, because He said He will never leave or forsake us--He is with us constantly, (Hebrews 13:5).

As we follow after holiness, we can see the Lord, (Hebrews 12:14). To the end that we will not see Jesus in our dreams, Satan tries to use certain tactics. At the same time, however, there are some natural conditions which can disturb sleep too. Before considering solutions to sleep/dream problems, we will broadly examine some of their causes and determine whether they are essentially natural, or spiritual.

Natural Causes of Sleep Disturbance

1) Lifestyle

How we behave and carry ourselves:

Our form of conversation--our manner of living practised during the day--can determine whether we will enjoy our sleep or not. If we have bad manners, bad habits, sins, or use profanity, these forms of behaviour invite or activate evil forces of darkness which can most easily disturb us during sleep (again, because we're most vulnerable then). What one sows during the day, he may, in a sense, reap in the night.

A person who sins is abased in sleep so that he may see the darkness, the fruit, of his sins. He is dealt with in sleep so that he may acknowledge the error of his ways, and repent. And the more highly he lifts himself up against the knowledge of God, the more deeply will he sink into the dark valley of sleep.

Isaiah 57:20-21 But the wicked are like the troubled sea, when it cannot rest, whose waters cast up mire and dirt. There is no peace, saith my God, to the wicked.

There is no peaceful sleep for sinners. They can't rest because their sins (mire and dirt) trouble them.

Forms of entertainment:

The movies and television programs we watch; the literature we read; the music we listen to; the friends or acquaintances we entertain; any and all other amusements we indulge throughout our daytime hours, may do a repeat performance in our minds during the night seasons--and that, perhaps, in a morbid version.

Food and drug consumption:

Unwise or unhealthy consumption of foods or drugs, particularly before bedtime, can disturb our sleep, and might also affect our dreams. This is especially true when we deviate from our normal habits.

Uncomfortable surroundings:

An uncomfortable bed; unsuitable blanket, pillow, or sleepwear; inappropriate headboard decorations; the room or immediate surroundings in a jumble or mess: these obviously might disturb one's sleep. Of course, if a person does not have control over these circumstances, if he has no choice but must sleep in such conditions, the grace of God can abound toward him and help him sleep in peace, (Romans 5:20).

Inconsistencies in daily activities:

One week on the night shift, the next week on the day shift; one month in the office, the next month in the field; a business meeting on Monday night in New York City, a seminar on Wednesday afternoon in Dallas, a convention on Thursday morning in Los Angeles: such deviations, instead of a regular routine, wear and tear a person as a whole, more than they should allow. One is thereby constantly picking up all kinds of spirits, new images and sounds in his mind, new "presences," and new physical surroundings. Doubtless to some degree his sleep and dreams will adversely respond thereto.

A person can habituate himself to an inconsistent schedule, but even then his sleep can become disturbed. The only exception is when one is anointed to serve God under these conditions.

2) Illness

Physical illness:

Physical illnesses can affect a person's dreams in two basic ways: physiologically, and psychologically. A physical problem must ultimately answer to the brain mechanism which houses the thought life. To greater or lesser degrees, sicknesses may affect the brain's functions and, consequently, the dreams.

When a person is physically sick, his self-concept too may thereby be affected to a degree. This also might influence his dreams. As a man thinketh, so might his dreams be; or so might he be in his dreams, (Proverbs 23:7a).

Emotional illness:

Emotional illnesses can more seriously and dramatically affect dreams. There are various kinds and degrees of emotional problems, and an innumerable amount of causes. Psychologists are largely helpless in discovering and healing such illnesses at the roots because the spiritual arena, which they generally ignore, is largely involved.

A person's spirit often has been wounded by traumatic experiences. Rejections, condemnations, mental shocks, unhappy childhood memories, and a great host of other possible injuries suffered and sustained by the heart can become roots of neuroses, aberrations, unforgiveness, and sins. These seek expression through illness in the body, illness in the mind (including the personality), and even through ill forms of dreams.

In the more serious cases, people seldom get a good night's rest. They might spend a lot of money seeking professional help, and might even become dependent on chemical substances--with or without a doctor's prescription, and with or without Jesus' permission.

Anointed ministers and Spirit-filled Christians are not automatically exempt from these problems. There are many Christians, as well as non-Christians, who suffer from nightmares, oppressions, bedwetting of one form or another, or a number of other unpleasant experiences during sleep. They may be caused by subconscious anxieties seeking to manifest while the natural body and mind rest. But demonic spirits can be the cause of these also.

But thank God we are not without help. God has provided in Christ all things that pertain unto life, (2Peter 1:3). He is able to subdue all things under His feet, and in Jesus Christ old things are passed away and all things are become new.

Spiritual Causes of Sleep Disturbance

1) Godlessness

If a person has not accepted Jesus Christ as his personal Lord and Saviour, he is without God in the earth, even though he might adhere to a religion. His eyes are blinded to the truth of the Gospel (2Corinthians 4:4), and therefore, his dreams are unyielded to God's peace, which comes through the Blood of Christ:

Ephesians 2:1-2, 12-14 (niv) As for you, you were dead in your transgressions and sins, in which you used to live when you followed the ways of this world and of the ruler of the kingdom of the air, the spirit who is now at work in those who are disobedient... Remember that at that time you were separate from Christ excluded from citizen-

ship in Israel and foreigners to the covenants of the promise, without
hope and without God in the world. But now in Christ Jesus you who
once were far away have been brought near through the Blood of
Christ. For He Himself is our peace.

Through Christ we have access to peaceful sleep, for so
He gives His beloved sleep, (Psalms 127:2). Without
Christ, one is unable to see the Light because the prince of
the power of the air, the ruler of the darkness of this
world, the devil, works and lords over the disobedient.

2) Satan

There are various ways through which Satan attempts to
enter into people's lives and "demonize" them. This does
not necessarily mean that they are owned or possessed by
the devil, but that they are to some degree oppressed by
him. One person may be more demonized than another, or
he may be more demonized in a certain area. As far as
concern dreams, Satan may attempt to steal, kill, or
destroy in one or more of the following ways:

Curses declared over a person:

Curses can be declared over a person. When a person
has a curse placed upon him, evil spirits are specifically
dispatched to torment him. The commission may or may
not include the dream area, but it will probably affect it.
Curses generally come in two ways. A person can inherit
the evil spirits which operated in the lives of his
predecessors much as he can inherit their diseases, traits,
or possessions. A person can also have enemies practising
witchcraft against him and releasing evil words (spells)
into his life.
Both of these kinds of curses can be powerful,
depending upon many considerations. But the inherited
curses are usually more powerful. The wicked spirits
involved in inherited curses know a person's ancestors and

present relatives, and possibly portions of his future. Therefore, they know some, if not all, of his weak points, and are usually quite settled in their strongholds, and are not easily expelled. When curses are finally destroyed by the power of the Blood of Jesus Christ, the person's dreams, as well as his real life, will experience a marked healing.

Demonic spirits:

Demons (also called devils, evil spirits, and wicked spirits) can disturb a person's sleep too. When they operate through curses they are more effective, but often Satan himself commissions evil spirits to torment people.

Sometimes demonic spirits may be sent forth to establish strongholds in a person's life, perhaps in a specified area. And sometimes they simply walk or fly around through many different homes and lives, seeking whom they may oppress. They seek comfort in places where the Holy Spirit's anointing is not present. If we go to sleep without God's presence, we are open to being visited and disturbed in our sleep by a demon, if there is one nearby. Of course, we can just cast him out in the Name of Jesus and go back to sleep with God's presence.

Physical objects:

Physical objects through which spiritual darkness has been transmitted can be a source of disturbance in our lives. Ornaments or souvenirs with which we decorate our homes should be discreetly, if not prayerfully, chosen. Not everything is attached to spirits, but we do want to be wise and use caution to some degree.

Some of the more questionable objects which may more easily become a point of contact with evil spirits are: posters and other images of actors, musicians, and other famous entertainers who are not saved, (they may be de-monized--again, some more than others); posters, paintings, or statuettes exhibiting sensuality or nakedness; weird, lewd, or immoral items; spears, swords, knives, guns, and similar wall hangings; dolls, masks, figures, and other things with eyes; statues, candles, incense, and other religious articles which do not exalt Jesus Christ; family heirlooms, mementos, and "personal things" which belonged to your parents, grandparents, or ancestors.

In some cases, a certain piece of furniture can be a channel for evil spirits. A wise woman of God once told me that she saw two demons in the knots of wood grain in an old wooden chest. In that case, one could pray and rebuke the demons or throw the chest out. She threw it out.

The colors of the walls in a person's home may occasionally attract a certain type of spirit. Even the anointing of the Holy Spirit can, at times, be particular about colors. Perhaps with a purpose in mind, God might tell you to paint a room another color, or to just paint it again the same color.

These truths are not to be feared, and they are not to be taken to one or another extreme. One might overly question or scrutinize every object in his home, or he might completely ignore these points--these are the two extremes. The safe "middle ground" is in that if one of the points mentioned here bears witness with one's spirit, or if in prayer God directs Him, he then can proceed with whatever actions he knows are best.

Whether or not you are disturbed in your sleep, be open to the Holy Spirit's wisdom and leading in this area. If there is a problem, He will reveal to you where it's coming from and how to deal with it. But He doesn't only respond to problems. He may speak in this regard because He has a new thing in store for you and wants your natural life to be as conducive to His new anointing as possible.

Some Common Problems

1) Insomnia

This is a condition in which a person cannot sleep. Most of the time the cause is worry, anxiety, or emotional stress. Demons may or may not be the cause. One should read the Bible, pray, and anoint himself in the Name of Jesus so that he may be healed.

Serious illness is occasionally the cause of insomnia. God can heal all of the causes and symptoms miraculously by His power. If one trusts Him completely, it will be done for him according to his faith, (Matthew 9:29). If he consults a physician, or resorts to tranquilizers, it should be under the direction of Jesus, the Great Physician.

2) Sleep-Talking

A person's mind or spirit can become so involved in a dream that his physical body becomes involved too. What he speaks while sleeping may or may not be intelligible, and may or may not be inspired by God. Actually this is not a problem but only a natural function which some people experience more than others.

Before going to sleep, we should pray with the spirit and with the understanding (according to 1Corinthians 14:13-15), and make confessions of faith that we will dream godly dreams and speak godly words, if any, in our sleep. Such words may be worth noting and recording if one believes God is revealing something by them. When the words are confusing or disturbing, an underlying worry or demon might be the cause.

3) Sleep-Walking

Here too, a person can become so involved in a dream that his physical body becomes involved too. With adults, excessive concern over unresolved matters is usually the cause. However, wicked spirits have been known to influence people's actions during sleep as well as their thoughts. Obviously, the more extreme the problem, the more earnestly the person should pray, even with the help of others. And when sleep-walking occurs, the person should not be awakened abruptly.

Children walk in their sleep more often than adults, and with them it's usually not serious. This happens because they are not yet fully able to distinguish dreaming from reality, and therefore, they cannot fully control their bodies while sleeping. The parents should prayerfully "mother" the child's spirit with their spirit during this experience, guiding him either to rest fully and normally, or to awaken fully and normally.

The child is a part of the parent's body, so the parent should keep his "body" under subjection to the Holy Spirit. He should cast down every high thing that exalts itself against the knowledge of God, or that seeks to divert from the normal, healthy course of behaviour and thought. He should bring into captivity every thought and action to the obedience of Christ, (2Corinthians 10:5; 1Corinthians 9:27a).

4) Bedwetting

Children can be taught during the day how to control their bodies during the night, so that after diapers are no longer used, the bladder can remain under control. Chronic bedwetting for which there is not apparent natural cause requires special anointed prayers for healing.

As with most sleep problems, bedwetting has physical, emotional, or spiritual causes, or any combination of these--especially with adults. We can command our bodily organs to become subject to our prayers, and anoint ourselves in the Name of the Lord. If necessary, we can also cast out a demon, or just not drink anything before bedtime.

5)   Wet Dreams

In the case of "wet dreams" (when semen is emitted during sleep), sexual dreams are usually the causes. Demonic spirits are usually behind such dreams, and in such cases they are known as *succubi*. We should immediately and boldly resist the evil dream and "will" ourselves to awaken--then rebuke the devil in the Name of Jesus.

In this type of evil dream, we should awaken to rebuke the devil because he is more directly trying to influence the physical body then. In dreams with mental thoughts only (dreams without the actual presence of evil spirits) we may at times take evil thoughts captive without necessarily waking up.

6)   Sexual Dreams

When a person dreams that he is having sex, it may be a simple scene in his mind, or it may be a real experience of a spiritual presence on his flesh body. In the former case, he should determine to take authority over his dream-thoughts and order them aright. He can cause himself to wake up in order to do this, or he can do this while he is still sleeping.

In the latter case, an evil spirit is actually trying to engage in sex with him while he sleeps. This kind of demon is called a *succubus*, (the singular form of *succubi*). The Latin word from which this is derived literally means "to lie under," (*sub:* "under," and *cubare:* "lie"). It also means "strumpet" (prostitute), "supplanter," and "rival." From this definition, we can clearly see that the devil (our enemy and rival) tries to supplant (unfairly take the place of) the human sex partner which the Lord has for us. And that's the same things which prostitutes do.

It may be that single people are more vulnerable to this type of demonic oppression than couples because they are not satisfying their sexual needs naturally. However, it may also be that the sexual problems of those who engage in sex on a regular basis, even those of married couples, may be attributable to jealous succubi.

In addition, these demons can also employ deceiving spirits to show seductive, illicitly sexual scenes to the dreamer's mind. By so doing, he deceives the dreamer into believing that he is simply entertaining a meaningless fantasy, when in fact he is gratifying the demon's sexual lusts. A wet bed can be evidence that this is an actual experience and not just a dream.

Succubi can assume either male or female forms, depending upon the person's sexual orientation and preference. Female ones attempt to visit men as they sleep, and male ones attempt to visit women as they sleep. Persons with homosexual tendencies might be visited by those assuming the form of a person of the same sex. And persons who commit bestiality (sexual acts with animals) might be visited by beast-like succubi. See how sophisticated the devil's manipulatory strategies can be?

These kinds of demonic visitations can come forcibly and without any disguise, in which case it is easy to discern that it is evil and that we should resist it. They can also come subtly, with a pleasant sense and a promise to gratify one's sexual needs, in which case we require greater spiritual discernment.

The unsaved are at a loss for help to resist these and all other kinds of demonic oppressions unless and until they commit their lives to the Lord Jesus Christ. Christians, on the other hand, always have the Holy Spirit as a "Standby" to alert them to spiritual warfare at the enemy's approach.

John 14:26a (amp) But the Comforter (Counselor, Helper, Intercessor, Advocate, Strengthener, Standby), the Holy Spirit, Whom the Father will send in My Name, [in My place, to represent Me and act on My behalf], He will teach you all things.

If an evil spirit comes to oppress you in your sleep, simply begin calling upon "The Blood of Jesus! in the Name of Jesus!" while you're still asleep. As you awaken, continue rebuking the foe that way and lay your hands on your head, your body, or anywhere else you may have felt, seen, or heard him, including your bed, your spouse, your floor, or anywhere else in the room.

This type of attack of the enemy may occur once or twice and then desist after you resist him. But if it persists, then you know a succubus is on a mission to own you, and you have a season of serious spiritual warfare at hand.

You will need to employ all God's weapons at your disposal (the Word of God, the Name of Jesus, the Blood of Jesus, the whole armour of God, the Holy Spirit, the ministry of angels, the Holy Communion Table, the laying on of hands with anointing oil and other points of contact, speaking with other tongues, the intercessory prayers of God's people on your behalf, fasting, and anything and everything else the Word of God provides for your victory), until you get the victory! And Jesus will be with you all the way through to make sure you win. He will deliver you from the strong enemy. Remember, the battle is not yours, but the Lord's.

7) Snoring

This is a hoarse, rattling sound made by the breathing apparatus during sleep. It is caused by relaxed muscles in the throat through which air must force itself into the lungs. Sometimes the position in which a person sleeps constricts certain throat muscles and causes the snoring.

This doesn't occur with everybody, and it isn't a dangerous condition. Only under special circumstances might it become dangerous because sometimes the throat muscles don't allow enough air into the lungs. This causes a lack of oxygen in the blood and in the brain, and the result may be disturbed sleep and aberrant dreams. When a person is snoring loudly, people usually comment, "He's sound asleep." Actually the opposite may be the case.

8) Nightmares

These are perverted and tormenting dreams. Whatever their causes, nightmares should be brought into captivity to the obedience of Christ. Usually demons cause them, therefore a person is to awaken and claim "The Blood of Jesus, in the Name of Jesus" in order to rebuke them.

Unpleasant experiences of the past which have never been fully committed unto the Lord and healed can be the root causes of nightmares too. Confronting and captivating our traumas and fears, perhaps with the aid of anointed counsel, can help old things to pass away and all things to become new, (2Corinthians 5:17).

9) Paralysis

One awakens from sleep and is conscious but the physical body is not yet fully awake and is unable to move for a few moments. Some functions of the brain, hence of the body, awaken later than others. This isn't dangerous or serious, and it doesn't happen every night or to everyone.

I have experienced this many times over the years, especially during adolescence. In my experience, I have learned that while this is occurring the spiritual eyes can be opened and spiritual discernment can be keen, whether the person is a Christian or not. I had experienced this countless times before being born-again. Each time it occurred, I was tormented by evil spirits and even saw, heard, and felt them. I was helpless against them.

After being saved, sanctified, and filled with the Holy Ghost, I still experienced this, and continued to be disturbed by evil spirits. Even now they tend to want to disturb my sleep once in awhile. But I always claim "The Blood of Jesus" against them with the voice of my spirit man and calmly awaken in victory. I have also begun to see angels of God when this temporary paralysis occurs. I no longer fear and panic when this happens because I know that I'm in control now, though now it occurs quite rarely.

A young Christian girl testified that she had experienced this paralysis while trying to wake up one morning. She saw, heard, and felt evil spirits playing musical instruments and laughing in her home. Her parents were involved in witchcraft at that time, which probably opened the door to the devil in that home. (All kinds of sins can open the door to the devil in people's lives to some degree, though he doesn't always come in abruptly. But non-Christian spiritual practises are the most inviting to him.)

This girl tried moving her body to awaken fully but it took several moments. She said she was afraid and felt helpless. I prescribed "The Blood of Jesus" as I'd learned from two incontrovertible sources: the Word of God, and experience.

10)   Coma

This is a deep, prolonged, unhealthy state of unconsciousness caused by alcoholism, diseases, injuries to the head, or other works of Satan--natural or spiritual. Medical attention is virtually helpless here because it does not acknowledge the spiritual realm and the true enemy.

Anointed prayers for those in a coma are the only avenue through which resurrection power can be imparted. The person's spirit is still in him and, therefore, he can acknowledge and respond to God's Word. Teaching tapes, confessions of faith, anointed prayers, and prophecies can minister unto the person and revive his mortal flesh. There's hope for the coma victim only in the power of Jesus Christ.

How Can We Enjoy Sleep?

Supernatural blessings and healings from God are available, but there is also practical knowledge and wisdom from God. First of all, once you know what's disturbing your sleep, often the remedy is obvious. Secondly, you do not always have to consciously pray or do something in order to receive God's help. By simply obeying basic truths, many problems are automatically solved.

1) Basic Deliverance

Abiding by God's Ways:

Proverbs 3:21, 24 My son, let not them depart from thine eyes: keep sound wisdom and discretion. When thou liest down, thou shalt not be afraid: yea, thou shalt lie down, and thy sleep shall be sweet.

When you obey God's Word and live in righteousness and true holiness, God's peace will be in your life. You'll lie down to sleep and none shall make you afraid. The Lord Himself will rid evil forces out of your presence (Leviticus 26:6), even as you sleep.

Prayer:

Isaiah 26:3 Thou wilt keep him in perfect peace, whose mind is stayed on Thee: because he trusteth in Thee.

Psalms 3:4-5 I cried unto the Lord with my voice, and He heard me out of His Holy Hill. Selah. I laid me down and slept; I awaked; for the Lord sustained me.

As our minds are stayed on the Lord through crying unto Him, worshipping Him in spirit and in truth, or other kinds of prayers, He keeps us in perfect peace and sustains us in sleep.

Understanding the dream mechanism:

A lot of times, Christians like to lay everything off on God as an excuse not to study and work. Some people say, "It's all up to God anyway. If God wants to help me in this area, He will--and if not, He won't." Ultimately these statements are true, but God helps us through the knowledge and understanding He makes available to us according to truth--whether it is found in His unadulterated Word or in scientific facts. True science always agrees with the Holy Bible. God's Word only repudiates "sciences" falsely so-called, (1Timothy 6:20).

Proverbs 24:3-6 Through wisdom is an house builded; and by understanding it is established: And by knowledge shall the chambers be filled with all precious and pleasant riches. A wise man is strong; yea, a man of knowledge increaseth strength. For by wise counsel thou shalt make thy war: and in multitude of counsellors there is safety.

Let's learn some things about the basic workings of dreams, such as are shared in this study. This is a part of God's wisdom through which He will help us in this area, for the Bible says, "Through knowledge shall the just be delivered," (Proverbs 11:9b).

Keeping a consistent schedule:

Dramatically changing sleep hours, eating habits, daily schedules, and other major activities, can cause unpleasant sleep and dreams. This is particularly true when changing them too quickly. Conversely, a regular routine helps the sleep/dream experience to remain undisturbed. Even so, our schedules do not necessarily need to be strict and inflexible.

Ministers of the Gospel who are anointed to be instant in season and out of season need special supernatural help from God in this area. Being "instant in season and out of season" (2Timothy 4:2a) can mean "being in the spirit in the day and in the night." Travelling from city to city with an everchanging itinerary, they obviously require a special touch of God in order to stay healthy in every area of their lives.

Furnishing your home with decent items:

Job 11:13-19 If thou prepare thine heart, and stretch out thine hands toward Him; If iniquity be in thine hand, put it far away, and let not wickedness dwell in thy tabernacles. For then shalt thou lift up thy face without spot; yea, thou shalt be steadfast, and shalt not fear: Because thou shalt forget thy misery, and remember it as waters that pass away: And thine age shall be clearer than the noonday; thou shalt shine forth, thou shalt be as the morning. And thou shalt be secure, because there is hope; yea, thou shalt dig about thee, and thou shalt take thy rest in safety. Also thou shalt lie down, and none shall make thee afraid; yea, many shall make suit unto thee.

Yield your heart and your possessions unto the Lord-- let Him sanctify you wholly. Remove all indecent and immodest furnishings, decorations, and ornaments from your home. The Holy Spirit might direct you specifically in this, but if He doesn't, simply refuse anything whereby another (if not yourself) might stumble or be offended, (Romans 14:20-21).

Even if an item in the home is not housing evil spirits, if it is indecorous it deserves no place in our homes where Jesus is Lord. We should adorn our homes with modest amounts of simple items, and they may include Scripture verses or drawings of Bible messages. Of course, we don't have to go to any extremes.

When these things are taken care of, there's no spot and no wickedness in your tabernacle, there's also no fear. You'll be secure and rest in safety. You'll lie down and nothing shall make you afraid. This is a subtle yet significant factor involved in peaceful sleeping and dreaming.

2) Supernatural Deliverance

Anointed prayers of deliverance:

James 5:14-15 Is any sick among you? let him call for the elders of the church; and let them pray over him, anointing him with oil in the

Name of the Lord: And the prayer of faith shall save the sick, and the Lord shall raise him up; and if he have committed sins, they shall be forgiven him.

God is moving powerfully in these last days in the area of visions and dreams. Therefore, Satan comes to steal, kill, and destroy in this area, (John 10:10). In some cases, his attacks are quite serious, and we require an extranatural power to be set free. To this end, God often uses His anointed servants to pray for our deliverance. They may visit the home, or pray in a Church service, and perhaps lay anointed hands on the person's head in the Name of Jesus. The anointing power from the Holy Ghost will destroy the oppressing yokes and set the afflicted free so that they can sleep in heavenly peace, (Mark 16:13).

<u>Anoint the home</u>:

Anointing the household, the bedroom, and the bed, is a powerful form of prayer. On occasion, when the need arises, we may anoint our homes with oil, like that use in cooking. This simply means that we commit the home unto the Lord in a special prayer, and we acknowledge His presence by using oil as a point of contact.

With a small amount of oil on our hands we touch the main door of the home and pray that God's Spirit will reside and reign there. The bedroom may likewise be presented unto the Lord. The bed itself, especially the pillows and the headboard, may also be anointed and blessed in this way. The head(s) of the household should lead the prayer, and the entire family (those who live there) may also be present. The prayer order is to depend upon how the Holy Spirit may lead. The Church leaders may also conduct special prayers of this sort for their Church members.

At times, God might inspire a person to thus anoint his home by himself. At other times, He might instruct that a few certain Christians be present. But these kinds of prayers are occasional and not daily. Only in seasons of extreme spiritual warfare might God inspire or require daily prayers of this kind. By the anointing, the actual presence of God, yokes are destroyed, (Isaiah 10:27).

<u>A prayer for anointing the home</u>:

"Heavenly Father, we come before Your presence in the Name of Jesus, welcoming Your lordship here. As we anoint this home, this room, and this bed, we acknowledge this oil as a tangible type and point of contact of Your presence. By Your Holy Spirit, guide us in all of the affairs of our lives and of our dreams.

We thank You that Your mighty angels minister for us in this home at all times, day and night, providing protection, direction, blessing, and instruction in dreams. We thank You that Your whole armour equips us fully in spiritual warfare, and that the mighty Blood of Jesus reigns over each member of this home. As we sleep, we are in Your presence, and no weapon that is formed against us shall prosper.

We meditate in Your Word and fellowship with You, Lord, in the night seasons. Any message which You desire for us to receive, we are sensitive, yielded, and ready to obey. We awaken with a new song in our hearts to praise You, and we remember and understand the dreams You desire for us to understand.

We commit this home and all activities here, natural and spiritual, into Your hands. Keep the Body of Christ in perfect peace as our minds are stayed on You. Bind the devices of the devil, and fill our home with Your precious presence.

May Your holy people, O Lord, lay down in peace and sleep, knowing that You will make us to dwell in safety, and revive us with great refreshing. In the almighty Name of the Lord Jesus Christ of Nazareth, we pray. Amen."

The powerful Name of Jesus:

Philippians 2:9-11   Wherefore God also hath highly exalted Him, and given Him a Name which is above every name: That at the Name of Jesus every knee should bow, of things in Heaven, and things in earth, and things under the earth; And that every tongue should confess that Jesus Christ is Lord, to the glory of God the Father.

John 14:13-14   And whatsoever ye shall ask in My Name, that will I do, that the Father may be glorified in the Son. If ye shall ask any thing in My Name, I will do it.

Mark 16:17   And these signs shall follow them that believe; In My Name shall they cast out devils.

We should learn about and exercise the authority we have in the Name of Jesus as we walk after the Spirit. We will then be free from fear of spiritual matters. In dreams, we enter a spiritual dimension which is sometimes pleasant and sometimes scary. Even the words "spirit" and "spiritual" are often jarring and are turn-offs to many people. This is due to ignorance of their place and power in the spiritual realm through Jesus Christ. (Even the word "power" is often scary.)

The reason that there is fear of spiritual things is because the devil, a fallen angel, has worked overtime to draw a negative and frightening picture of the spirit world. He has often been able to do this through television, movies, books, myths, old wives' tales, and other media. Many people have allowed Satan to deceive them into thinking that he is powerful and that they are powerless. But the Holy Bible tells us that it's really the other way around.

Let's not shy away from spiritual things, but instead give ourselves unto them. The devil and all evil has been defeated by Jesus Christ's death, burial, and resurrection. Therefore now, in Christ Jesus, we have as much power and victory over Satan and all of his cohorts as Jesus has

(Ephesians 1:18-23), even over sickness, poverty, and spiritual death, (Galatians 3:13-14, 29).

As Christians, when we learn of our authority and rights in Jesus Christ, we'll enjoy greater victory in our lives, and we'll also enjoy and benefit more from our dreams. Also, if there are any thoughts or memories, recent or from long ago, which have not allowed us to have a pleasant sleep/dream life, those things will be healed because God's Word is life unto us and medicine to *all* our flesh, (Proverbs 4:22).

God wants us to have a healthy and prosperous dream life and to be totally free of worry, anxiety, fear, and undue concern of any kind. When we learn to trust Jesus in every area of our lives, we will begin to sleep in the peace of God which is rightfully ours. The God of peace shall be with us, (Philippians 4:9).

Don't let the sun go down without committing all your thoughts unto Jesus. Don't give the devil any place in your dreams, (Ephesians 4:26-27). Not giving everything to Jesus before sleeping can open the door to bad dreams.

Be anxious for nothing, and be careful for nothing, (Philippians 4:6). Cast all your cares, concerns, and petitions over on the Lord because He is the Good Shepherd of your soul, and He cares for you, (1Peter 2:25; 5:7). He is Jehovah-Shalom, the Lord our Peace, (Judges 6:24; Isaiah 9:6).

John 14:27 Peace I leave with you, My peace I give unto you: not as the world giveth, give I unto you. Let not your heart be troubled, neither let it be afraid.

Philippians 4:7 And the peace of God, which passeth all understanding, shall keep your hearts and minds through Christ Jesus.

Proverbs 3:5-6 (author's paraphrase) Trust (rest, even during sleep) in the Lord with all thine heart; and lean not unto thine own understanding. In all thy ways (thoughts and dreams) acknowledge Him, and He shall direct thy paths.

The Lord will also direct the paths your thoughts should take, even during the night seasons in dreams.

Chapter 4

Adventures in the Night Seasons

Job 4:13 In thoughts from the visions of the night,
when deep sleep falleth on men.

A lot of things are happening while we sleep--both inside of us and outside of us. Most of this activity we are not knowledgeable about while it's happening, and we do not even remember most of it. But we can still be safe from evil and blessed by God during this time. Our before-bedtime prayers are still active throughout our sleep, and the angels of God are still hearkening unto the voice of the Word of God which we have prayed, (Psalms 103:20).

Now the study of the workings of dreams, the different kinds of and experiences in dreams, and so forth, is an inexaustible one. This is true, not only because the Bible abounds in knowledge in this area from Genesis to Revelation, but also because the diversity of experiences possible and their various implications are virtually limitless. We will attempt here, for our purposes, to disclose and clarify some basic truths and to offer some insights which will help us to understand peculiar experiences.

The first and most important consideration is that the born-again human spirit attempts to enlighten and lead the mind. On the other hand, a sinner is not alive unto God in the spirit, and therefore is necessarily led by his own carnal, sinful nature.

The next important factor is that between the spirit and the mind there are some "gray areas." Therefore, the will of a born-again Christian can yield to the desires of God in his spirit, or to the desires of his carnal mind (if it's not totally submitted to God), or to one of those gray areas. We are a spirit, and we have a mind, but there's not a clear-cut distinction between the two. That's why possessing our souls (our minds) is a gradual process of renewing day by day.

Only the Word of God is sharp enough to pierce and divide asunder that which is of the mind and that which is of the spirit--only the Word of God can make a clear distinction between the mind and the spirit of a person, (Hebrews 4:12). Our own natural understanding isn't able to discern where to draw the line.

In sleep, the mind has a lot of thoughts and ideas it wants to repeat back to us. If we allow the mind to do this by itself, our dreams will be natural, unspiritual ones. Also, since the devil can work in the natural realm, we might thereby be giving him place in our dreams. We have got to bring all our natural minds into subjection to our spirits and let the latter instruct and lead the former.

Another important fact is that the spirit often performs a greater role than just communicating to the mind. A lot of times the spirit actually begins to speak for himself, surpassing the minds functions, or he might literally do something. When this happens, we may think it is only a dream, but it's more. This is an actual occurrence, an actual experience.

Your spirit is the real you, the inward man of the heart, (Romans 7:22). Your outer man (the mind, body, and senses) is the temple of the real you. So the inner man looks and sounds like the outer man (or rather, the outer man copies the inner man), and either of them can play the greater role in a dream. This is why we regard all our perceptions during sleep as dreams. But technically there is a difference between the spirit's operations and those of the mind during sleep.

When your inner man decides to function more directly and literally during sleep, it is not just a dream occurring because your spirit is a real person and not just another part of your mind. Again, there are some gray areas here because there are greater and lesser degrees of control which the spirit might choose to exercise over the mind during sleep.

Further, Jesus may manifest His lordship over the person's spirit in a supernatural way. When He does, his spirit and mind are more fully subjected to God's message via a supernatural dream. This too can be either a message to the mind inspired by God or an actual experience with God in the spirit. Here too, there is a "gray area" because the degree of God's presence can vary.

The best way to determine when your spirit is assuming

the major role in a dream is by determining his measure of influence over the dream content. While sleeping, if you realize that you can consciously form the dream you desire, it is your spirit instructing your mind. The more influence you can exert in the production of a dream, the more your spirit is directing the mind's functions. The dreams you produce in this way, whether you're a Christian or a sinner, give testimony of what are the desires of your heart, and of where you are spiritually.

In the foregoing chapters, we learned a lot about the mind's functions in dreams. In Chapter 8, *Supernatural Dreams and Trances,* we will explore experiences wherein God is more directly involved. In this current Chapter, we will view some of the ways which the spirit (of a born-again Christian) may behave during sleep.

Most of the time, the spirit of the person will simply illuminate the mind to God's wisdoms or to His leadings. But often he will surpass the mind and exercise his powers according to his measure of faith in the Word of God he has learned. Keep in mind that it is difficult to make a clear distinction between the various degrees of control our spirits may wield.

On the one end of our spirit's behaviour in sleep we border on natural thoughts. On the other end we border on the supernatural unction of God. In the middle ground, a wide range of experiences and exploits can be enjoyed. And as stated earlier, greater freedom and greater faith are at times exercised concerning some matters during this time, as opposed to during the waking hours. This is not the rule but only another avenue of faith.

Five Basic Activities

I have listed five basic kinds of activities in which our spirits may engage during sleep. They are: 1) Worship and Praise; 2) Intercessory Prayer; 3) Spiritual Warfare; 4) Petitioning the Lord; and 5) Self-Edification. Each enjoys a wide variety of applications and manifestations, and they may overlap one with another. The purpose of categorizing them here is to identify them, to define them with illustrations, to establish their validity in the Word of God, and to excite faith for these experiences.

1) Worship and Praise

Psalms 63:5-8 My soul shall be satisfied as with marrow and fatness; and my mouth shall praise Thee with joyful lips: When I remember Thee upon my bed, and meditate on Thee in the night watches. Because Thou hast been my help, therefore in the shadow of Thy wings will I rejoice. My soul followeth hard after Thee: Thy right hand upholdeth me.

We should worship God always. Even in sleep we can enjoy precious fellowship with the Lord and praise Him. Remember God's help. Remember how His wings have covered you as a hen gathers her chickens under her wings. The shadow of death poses no threat to him that abides under the shadow of the Almighty.

We can follow hard after Jesus, as He commands us to, and we can do so with our spirits in the night seasons. His right hand upholds us then as well as during the day. Remembering and meditating upon Him during sleep can bring great satisfaction to our souls. Marrow and fatness is nourishing, pleasant, and delicious, and He feeds us therewith as we revel in His presence.

Isaiah 26:9a With my soul have I desired Thee in the night; yea, with my spirit within me will I seek Thee early.

Isaiah 26:9a (tev) At night I long for You with all my heart.

We should desire, yearn, long for the Lord in the night seasons. If we can seek Him in dreams in a way exclusive to dreams, surely we can find Him in dreams in a way exclusive to dreams.

Psalms 77:6 (niv) I remembered my songs in the night. My heart mused and my spirit inquired.

Before bedtime, we can choose which songs we'll sing to God with our spirits during sleep, and we will remember them. In the night God's song should be with us, (Psalms 42:8). But if we don't retire with a song on our hearts, He can give us songs in the night, (Job 35:10). We can sing aloud *upon our beds!*, (Psalms 149:5).

Many times I have sung unto the Lord in other tongues, and also in English, and I have even danced in the spirit-- all of this while my natural body and mind slept. I would even awaken at times to find myself still praising God aloud. So this is more than just dreaming. This is actual singing and praising the Lord in the spirit--that is, with my spirit.

2) Intercessory Prayer

2Timothy 1:3 I thank God, Whom I serve from my forefathers with pure conscience, that without ceasing I have remembrance of thee in my prayers night and day.

1Thessalonians 3:10 Night and day praying exceedingly that we might see your face, and might perfect that which is lacking in your faith.

The spirit, the inner man of the heart, should continue in intercessions always--daily and nightly. Even while sleeping we may "stand in the gap" for others and be "touched" with the feeling of their infirmities and weaknesses, (Hebrews 4:15).

I have experienced spiritual groaning and travailing in intercession during sleep many times. Others' burdens would come upon me and I would receive an anointing to labour for them with the spirit. On occasion I would awaken, still travailing, and with the *mind of Christ* concerning those for whom I have prayed--that is, with the prophetic *word of the Lord* they require.

3)   Spiritual Warfare

Ephesians 6:10-18   Finally, my brethren, be strong in the Lord, and in the power of His might. Put on the whole armour of God, that ye may be able to stand against the wiles of the devil. For we wrestle not against flesh and blood, but against principalities, against powers, against the rulers of the darkness of this world, against spiritual wickedness in high places. Wherefore take unto you the whole armour of God, that ye may be able to withstand in the evil day, and having done all, to stand. Stand therefore, having your loins girt about with truth, and having on the breastplate of righteousness; And your feet shod with the preparation of the Gospel of peace; Above all, taking the shield of faith, wherewith ye shall be able to quench all the fiery darts of the wicked. And take the helmet of salvation, and the sword of the Spirit, which is the Word of God: Praying always with all prayer and supplication in the Spirit, and watching thereunto with all perseverance and supplication for all saints.

The whole armour of God includes the weapons of our warfare which we need for sleep. We need to wear the armour daily, and nightly, as the Israelites did while re-building the Temple at Jerusalem, (Nehemiah 4:9). The rulers of the darkness of this world, Satan and his cohorts, try to creep up on us in the night sometimes more than during the day. They realize that when people rest in physical sleep they usually rest their spiritual defenses as well.

The Bible shows us many instances of people being overcome overnight while they were asleep. As a result of spiritual slumbering (sin), spiritual beasts (demons) were able to devour God's own people, (Isaiah 56:9-10). The Nazarite Samson was overcome by his enemies while he slept, (Judges 16:19). Even our Lord Jesus was attacked by Satan while He was sleeping in the disciples' boat, (Matthew 8:23-27). The devil knew that his weapons could not prosper against Jesus while He was fully awake, so he thought he would attack Him with a great tempest out at sea as He slept. He soon found out Jesus wore all God's armour, all the time!

I too have been assaulted by evil spirits while asleep in ways I've never been attacked when awake. But the power of God has always seen me through so that the wicked one touches me not. With the shield of faith still operating in the night, we are able to stand against the wiles of the devil, resist his every attack, and quench all the fiery darts he launches against us. For ourselves or for others, we can wrestle and defeat all the devices of the devil. We are to war a good warfare always by praying always with all kinds of prayers--day prayers, and night prayers.

God fights a good fight in the night too. Even Elihu, one of Job's friends, knew that:

Job 34:20 (tev) **A man may suddenly die at night. God strikes men down and they perish; He kills the mighty with no effort at all.**

King Saul and his soldiers were penetrated by God's servant David as they slept, (1Samuel 26:12). Sisera was destroyed by God's handmaiden Jael while he slept, (Judges 4:21). King Belshazzar was overturned in the night as he slept, (Daniel 5:30). Even today many of God's enemies are being overturned (in one way or another) in the night seasons. The sleeping state is one during which spiritual powers--evil or good--can easily work.

In warfare during sleep we can still be strong in the Lord and in the power of His might. Just because we are asleep, that doesn't mean we must be defenseless. I usually start shouting "The Blood of Jesus!" against the devil. The voice of my spirit man repeatedly claims and commands the victory through the overcoming Blood of the Lamb of God, (Revelation 12:11). Eventually the devil will bow his knee. When we're willing to show him that we are determined to resist him no matter how long it takes, it won't take long. Having done all in battle, I'm able to stand--or rather, to sleep. Sometimes we've got to awaken to do spiritual battle, but it's not always necessary.

Interesting too, is that when we are receiving an important message in a dream, and a demon comes to interrupt or impede it, we shouldn't always rush to rebuke him. First of all, we should inquire of the Lord how to deal with each particular situation. But let us be open to the possibility that God might have us ignore the devil until we have received the full message in the dream. Otherwise we might destroy the "wheat" along with the "tares" (Matthew 13:24-30), that is, the good parts of a dream with the evil parts. Wheat and tares are very similar in appearance and can be difficult to distinguish.

If there is no urgency to rebuke a dream-bothering demon, and Jesus doesn't specifically instruct you to do so, see if the good seed will grow and appear until the harvest (when you wake up) knowing that the whole armour of God is upon you as you're sleeping. It may be that after you have received the full message, the demon is not there. The devil is a liar (John 8:44), and he might try to present an image that is not really there in order to get your attention away from God's message. If a demon is actually present, God may have you cast him out immediately, or after you have received His message.

The tares in a given dream may not be literal demons. They may simply be foolish and unnecessary natural thoughts. But in the midst of such kinds of dreams we might still find some wheat. So we don't want to root up the wheat before the time of harvest just to avoid entertaining some tares. As Jesus said, let both grow together until the harvest, at which time we can winnow the dream-thoughts, first binding the evil tares to burn them, then gathering the good wheat into the storehouse.

The angels (reapers, in Matthew 13:30, 39) are sent forth to minister for us in the area of winnowing our harvest of dream-thoughts. The more directly demons are involved in our dreams, the more directly will the angels become involved in the winnowing process. Conversely, when the tares are simply evil thoughts, the angels may not involve themselves too supernaturally, (unless, of course, God instructs them to regardless). We have power

over all the power of the enemy on whatever level of battle
we find ourselves.

God is faithful. He will not allow us to be overcome by
temptations to sin and attacks of the devil. Where sin and
Satan abound, the grace of God much more abounds so
that we will not only escape but also destroy the works of
the devil, (1Corinthians 10:13; Romans 5:20b; 1John 3:8).

4) Petitioning the Lord

**Psalms 6:6-9 I am weary with my groaning; all the night make I my
bed to swim; I water my couch with my tears. Mine eye is consumed
because of grief; it waxeth old because of all mine enemies. Depart
from me, all ye workers of iniquity; for the Lord hath heard the voice
of my weeping. The Lord hath heard my supplication; the Lord will
receive my prayer.**

In this psalm, David petitions the Lord for mercy,
strength, healing, and deliverance. He says the Lord
receives his prayer, therefore he must be praying in faith,
for without faith it is impossible to please God, or to
receive anything from Him, (Hebrews 11:6).

We too can petition the Lord all the night. With faith
our spirits will come boldly unto the Throne of Grace,
obtain mercy, and find grace to help in any time of need,
(Hebrews 4:16). If we have agreed with others in prayer
for our needs to be met, perhaps even had anointed hands
laid upon us, God's answers might manifest while we are
sleeping.

I've heard many testimonies of Christians waking up--in
the middle of the night, or in the morning--speaking in
tongues, healed, anointed, or knowing God's leading which
they required. This happens a lot of times after having
enjoyed an anointed Church service the night before. The
anointing of God's Spirit comes upon the congregation
then and begins a work in their lives--and throughout the
night He often completes that work.

Conviction may come upon a sinner in a Church service,

yet he might not accept Jesus Christ as his personal Lord and Saviour immediately. But that night he might dream of his lost condition, and might even catch a glimpse of Hell. He may awaken shouting, "Jesus, I repent! Save me!" This is because his spirit was convicted of sin and decided to instruct his mind to get saved. Therefore, this is more than just dreaming, it is actually confronting reality *in the night seasons* and being allowed to make choices about it.

In one anointed service, the preacher ministered right in from of me as I sat in one of the front seats. I was saying to myself, "I hope he prays for me. I wish he would lay hands on me and prophesy to me." Well, he didn't do it. But as I slept that night, my spirit stood up and came before him, and he then laid anointed hands upon me and prophesied.

On another occasion, a minister laid anointed hands upon my head, hands, and chest, and he prophesied to me. I felt a certain amount of fire come through his hands. As I slept that night, I felt that same fire upon where he had laid his hands. But then it intensified and even spread down into other parts of my body, especially into an area which had been afflicted. What the Holy Spirit began in the service through the minister's prayer for me, He completed that night as I slept.

On yet another occasion, a woman of God anointed me and prayed for me with groanings and spiritual travail. That night I experienced the same thing in sleep, only in a more intense anointing. I had perceived the anointing as she prayed for me the night before, but while sleeping I was able to see and feel that anointing more as it really was. Also, her prayer was intensified and I understood it more for what it really was.

In many wonderful meetings I've desired for God's servants to minister to me personally, perhaps even prophesy to me. Most of the time it hasn't happened. I know that many Christians desire the same thing. But the ministers can only minister to us personally and specifically to a limited degree in large meetings. However, in the spiritual realm the Holy Ghost Himself is ministering specifically to each one present much more so than meets the eye.

In the visions of the night I've often been visited and ministered unto by God's servants. Even some of my friends and neighbours have on occasion visited me in supernatural and in regular dreams providing me with wisdom and insights from the Lord. Other Christians have testified to me of having similar experiences. The Holy Spirit imparts to us just the word, the anointing, the direction, or other blessing which we needed. God's servants may or may not even be aware that He is using them to minister unto us in the spiritual dimension in this way.

5) Self-Edification

Psalms 4:4 Stand in awe, and sin not: commune with your own heart upon your bed, and be still. Selah.

While we are sleeping, but our hearts are awake, we should commune with our own selves and edify ourselves. Perhaps we should speak to ourselves in psalms, hymns, and spiritual songs which would bless us. As did Joshua, we should meditate on the Book of the Law (the Bible, God's Word) day and night.

Jude 20 But ye, beloved, building up yourselves on your most holy faith, praying in the Holy Ghost.

Praying in the Holy Ghost, with all kinds of prayers and supplications, always and without ceasing, necessarily involves the night seasons. And meditating and confessing God's Word as we sleep helps us to edify and build ourselves up on our most holy faith.

As the mind can consciously decide what to think about during the day, so it may be able to choose what to think on in the night, when the body is sleeping. Since natural things are less demanding in that state, and the spiritual realm is more open, we can weigh some things which have been on our minds and make judgments about them.

Dream-thoughts do not need to be directly inspired by the Holy Spirit in order to be valid and true. A mind which has been renewed to the Word of God can think in scriptural terms and ideas, make decisions, and instruct itself in the ways of God in the night seasons, (Psalms 16:7). God commanded Joshua to meditate on the Book of the Law day and night in order that *he* may observe what to do to prosper, (Joshua 1:8).

The will of a man has the right to determine the way his thoughts will go. And if his will is set on following the Master, his thoughts too will follow after godliness, truth, and understanding, even in the night seasons. Then shall he understand the fear of the Lord and have good success; then may he prosper and be in health, even as his soul prospers.

Chapter 5

Dream Recall and Interpretation

Daniel 2:26 Art thou able to make known unto me the dream which I have seen, and the interpretation thereof?

Daniel 2:3-5 I have dreamed a dream, and my spirit was troubled to know the dream... The thing is gone from me.

King Nebuchadnezzar of Babylon confessed this after having received a dream from the Lord. The dream troubled him and kept him up, but he could not make anything of it or even recall it.

Daniel 2:22 He revealeth the deep and secret things: He knoweth what is in the darkness, and the light dwelleth with Him.

The Prophet Daniel spoke this when God had revealed to him King Nebuchadnezzar's dream and its interpretation. He here refers to dreams as *deep secrets* which are *hidden in darkness* (or, we might say, in *subconsciousness*). He knew that dream-thoughts repose in the back of men's minds, and that God's light can repossess them. Daniel had a great understanding of dream processes, (Daniel 1:17).

It is a very common occurrence among all peoples everywhere that we dream and forget our dreams. They may disturb us, awaken us, and often keep us from going back to sleep--all without our understanding or even remembering them. Be they spiritual dreams or natural-- with important insights or unimportant ones--they have troubled all of us at one time or another. Even Daniel himself, a prophet of God with an excellent spirit, and one greatly beloved of the Lord, was occasionally troubled and went through changes as a result of his dream experiences, (Daniel 7:28).

I believe that supernaturally-inspired dreams--dreams which God makes a special effort to deliver to us--give us less of a problem in recall and interpretation. His light is more present to help us then. However, all dreams, natural and spiritual ones, need to be guarded against natural functions which desire to quench spiritual revelations. Practical knowledge in this area can help us to remember our dreams whether or not they are inspired supernaturally.

Dream Recall

While waking up from sleep, carnal thoughts and functions are reactivated and they tend to smother, subjugate, or otherwise stifle dream-thoughts. That's why most dreams are hard to remember. Natural dreams often divulge information which the conscious mind doesn't want to acknowledge--whether they are incomprehensible sillinesses, or valid facts. Yet spiritual dreams can divulge information from the Holy Spirit, which is always valid, and the natural mind often tries to quench these too.

When undesirable dream-thoughts such as unpleasant memories, vain imaginations, or even exhortations from the Lord, are repeatedly hindered from reaching consciousness, they may be revised either by the subconscious mind, or by God Himself. The Spirit of God, and our own spirit, may persist to reveal such thoughts intending to teach, heal, or help us somehow. This is one reason why we have recurring dreams. We might reject the first version, so another is produced, one which may be less offensive to the conscious mind.

Fleshly thoughts war against spiritual thoughts because they are contrary the one to the other, (Galatians 5:17). The carnal mind is enmity against God because it is not subject to the mind of Christ and the laws of God, neither indeed can it be, (Romans 8:7). The more spiritually-minded we become, the easier it will be for our wills to accept and to remember dream-thoughts inspired of the Spirit.

While dreaming, you may be able to note some highlights or distinct features and retain them, carrying them with you until you awaken. As you begin to wake up, you can pull those dream-thoughts along with you into full consciousness.

However, this can disturb, interfere with, and possibly alter the dream content. Your will is involved here and may decide to edit or revise the messages as he pleases. You might prefer to pray in faith (before going to sleep) that you will retain the desired dream-thoughts. Even so, it is possible to begin retaining dream-thoughts while they are yet being dreamed.

There are deep mysteries in our spirits where God abides and they often seek expression in dreams. When we awaken, we may immediately begin to speak mysteries in the spirit (according to 1Corinthians 14:2) and proceed to interpret them, (according to verse 13 of that Chapter). If there is anything worth remembering from your dreams, it might easily be recalled this way.

Proverbs 20:5   Counsel in the heart of man is like deep water; but a man of understanding will draw it out.

The Lord gives us counsel, deep water, in the night seasons, (Psalms 16:7). By praying with the spirit and with the understanding, we can draw out God's counsel from *the deep*. Spiritual mysteries, secret knowledge--yes, pearls of great price--are planted in us by the Lord. When our spirits pray in other tongues, they often tell those secrets so that they are no longer secret. Praying with other tongues means praying with our spirits, and praying with our understanding means praying in our natural regular language.

When you want to remember a dream which you believe was of God, pray in other tongues while seeking the lost dream with your mind. The Holy Spirit will help you here because you are talking in His language, (Romans 8:26). And once the dream is recalled, the same Spirit--by the same method--will help in its interpretation.

Also, as we mentioned in Chapter 2, we can speak in other tongues before bedtime and begin to call forth mysteries. Then while we're asleep, our spirits may continue in that vein and produce dreams which feature and possibly enlarge upon those mysteries. Isn't that interesting? I have enjoyed many blessings, insights, and supernatural experiences in dreams after lengthy sessions of praying with the spirit.

While praying with my spirit and with my understanding before going to sleep, I receive thoughts, impressions, ideas, words, and images. When I go to sleep, those same things may be repeated in dreams--only now presented as seen through the eyes of Jesus. And if I have a specific burden or petition on my heart, it too can be appraised in a dream following prayer. That's one reason why I pray before going to sleep.

John 14:26 But the Comforter, which is the Holy Ghost, Whom the Father will send in My Name, He shall teach you all things, and bring all things to your remembrance, whatsoever I have said unto you.

John 16:13 Howbeit when He, the Spirit of Truth, is come, He will guide you into all truth: for He shall not speak of Himself; but whatsoever He shall hear, that shall He speak: and He will shew you things to come.

You can lean upon the ministry of the Holy Spirit during sleep. As Jesus said, He will teach you all things (all you need to know), He will guide you into all truth (guide your thoughts into God's will for you), He shows you things to come (portions of the future He intends you should know), He reminds you of God's words (the current words you need, *rhema*).

Before going to sleep, we should praise and thank the Lord that His Spirit teaches and guides us in the night seasons and at times shows us future events. Then we should ask to remember and interpret what He wants us to. (In Chapter 2, we have shared several verses from the Bible which are appropriate to confess in order that we may remember and benefit from our dreams.)

By faith, a person can declare what the Bible says about him, and tailor his confession to the remembering of his dreams:

"Heavenly Father, I thank You that I am blessed with all spiritual blessings in heavenly places in Christ. I have the mind of Christ. The eyes of my understanding are enlightened. You visit me in the night and speak in dreams. The Holy Spirit brings all dreams to my remembrance as they are required. I confess by faith that I recall perfectly the dreams You inspire, and that my mind is completely conducive to them. In the Name of Jesus. Amen."

Two or three believers (Christians who believe this is proper) may pray together asking and believing that an inspired dream will be recalled, (Matthew 18:19-20). In the presence of God, they can agree that the dreamer will remember his forgotten dream, and it shall be done for them:

"Lord, we two (or three) gather together in Your Name and know that You are in our midst. We each touch the other's faith in agreement that this dream which one of us has dreamed will be recalled and interpreted accurately by the help of Your Holy Spirit. We believe we receive and call it done, in Jesus' Name. Amen."

By the laying on of anointed hands, a dream inspired by the Holy Spirit can be recalled by the same Spirit. If the anointing can cause a divinely suggested dream to come (as we saw in Chapter 4), then surely it can cause us to remember such a dream. And the dreamer may not even know he has dreamed an important dream. While receiving prayer by the laying on of anointed hands for some other purpose, the Holy Spirit can bring to his remembrance a dream which--until now--he hadn't realized he had dreamed.

With or without a specific kind of prayer, a hindrance in the mind (a yoke, we might say) can be destroyed because of the anointing. Then the needed dream-thoughts will be free to arise and shine for their light has come.

Before bedtime is a good time to "loose" desired dream-thoughts by faith and to "bind' undesirable ones, according to the prayer principle of *binding and loosing:*

Matthew 18:18 Verily I say unto you, Whatsoever ye shall bind on earth shall be bound in Heaven: and whatsoever ye shall loose on earth shall be loosed in Heaven.

To recall a forgotten dream, one may pray:

"I bind and rebuke any force of darkness attempting to obstruct my dream from my view, in the Name of Jesus. I cast down lying imaginations and bring into captivity every dream-thought I've just now dreamed. I command my mind and its dreams to obey Christ, and in His Name I stir up, call forth, and loose into my conscious memory, that dream which the Lord inspired."

This can also be prayed when we awaken, as explained in Chapter 4, under *Spiritual Warfare.*

While praying to remember a forgotten dream, we can guess at what it involved until something bears witness, fits the picture, or comes into view: "Did it involve me, my Church, or my family? Did it involve Christians, or sinners, or both? Did it involve books, or buildings, or money, or other objects? Did it involve this color or that color, this mood or that mood, this idea or that idea?

Something is bound to click just right if the Spirit is helping you. And once a dream-thought is recalled, others usually follow. Then you can proceed to interpret.

When you remember one or two details of a dream, you may speak it out, write or draw it out, or even act it out. Once you get the wheels in motion, your memory can build momentum and divulge the whole dream. Some things need to be worked at if they will work, but once activated may prove active indeed.

A good way to seek after a lost dream is to penetrate the spiritual eyes into the seeming darkness looking into the unknown by faith. With the natural eyes closed, the spiritual eyes can stretch on out there endeavouring to restore to view dream-thoughts which have disappeared. Jesus said, "Seek, and you shall find," (Matthew 7:7).

A spiritual dream which we do not remember may be saying, "Seek me, and you shall see me. If you see me when I am taken from you, you shall receive my message; but if not, it shall not be so," (2Kings 2:10, author's paraphrase). Again, any leading of the Spirit to leave it alone should be carefully heeded.

We should also have near our beds a pencil and notebook or a tape recorder to record our dreams as soon as we recall them. By demonstrating to God an expectant attitude, we show Him how eager we are to fellowship with Him. The very act of placing these items near us as we sleep indicates that we desire and expect to remember our dreams. And realizing the fact that we dream several dreams every night anyway, whether or not we remember those dreams, should inspire us to diligently seek the dreams He is doubtless giving.

We should desire and expect to remember the dreams God inspires. A right relationship with God frees us from condemnation and guilt from sin, therefore we should not fear and resist His messages in dreams. In fact, as we are zealous to receive from Him during the day, so should we be during the night seasons.

The Bible too, and Scripture-based reference books, should be kept near at hand ready to be consulted. No matter how gifted a Christian may be in spiritual things, he should compare his revelations with those of other Christians, especially with those in the Bible. He might come to understand the full interpretation of his revelation through that which has been previously revealed. Daniel understood *by books*--by studying previous writings--the number of years appointed for Israel's return from Babylonian captivity, (Daniel 9:2).

God's people, and the revelations He gives us, are often destroyed for a lack of knowledge, (Hosea 4:6). Noble are those who, like the Bereans in Acts 17, search the Scriptures diligently. Noble are those who compare spiritual things with Scriptural to interpret the things that are given to us of God.

As a rule, when a dream is inspired by the Spirit of God, we will awaken immediately when it ends. God wants us to remember it, so He usually doesn't want us to keep on sleeping, at least not right away. Immediately after the dream, He may exhort us, "Get up right now and write it down or record it, otherwise you will forget it. Then you may go back to sleep."

If you disobey the Lord in this, saying, "Don't worry, God, I won't forget it. I just don't want to get up right now," it's not very likely you'll remember it. Not just because of disobedience, but because--unless the Lord *really* helps you remember it--your following dreams will subjugate it. God wants us to remember the dreams He inspires, so He wakes us up, if only for a minute or two, as soon as they are disclosed.

When the Pharaoh of Egypt dreamed about seven years of plenty followed by seven years of famine, he immediately awoke. He went right back to sleep and dreamed the same message (only in different symbolism) and again immediately awoke, (Genesis 41:1-7). He also immediately remembered the dreams (verse 8), though he did not understand them. Clearly, these dreams were supernaturally inspired by God, as the events which followed affirm.

Also, in Genesis 40, two men, a butler and a baker, each had a dream pertaining to his own future. When Joseph, the anointed Dreamer, saw them in the morning, they were sad because they knew exactly what they had dreamed, only they didn't understand the meanings of their dreams. When Joseph asked them to tell him their dreams, they had no problem remembering them. Since it was morning, we may presume that they awoke immediately after dreaming and perhaps couldn't go back to sleep.

Whether or not this is so, both their dreams contained undeniable spiritual insight. They were disclosed with a supernatural element, for they involved the future, and they spoke messages which were irrefutably true, as was afterward affirmed.

Remembering that there are varying degrees of God's presence in dreams, let's understand that we will not always awaken immediately after having received simple wisdoms and basic insights in dreams. And often we will not even remember them. There's a whole array of spiritual revelations from the Lord which we can receive throughout the night without awakening and without even recalling them. But these may not even border on the supernatural. Yet obviously, we should pray that we will recall dreams which can help us in our real lives, even though they are ideas of our own minds instructing us in the night seasons.

The more directly God inspires us to dream a dream, the more directly He inspires us to awaken and recall the dream. Or He might just have us to awaken. During the following day, we may see or hear something which might remind us of something we dreamed the preceding night (or that morning). But usually, supernatural dreams are immediately awakened from and recalled. Again, this is the rule, with few exceptions.

There is an important point here about waking up. Normally, awakening from sleep occurs with the mind beginning to approach consciousness, the eyes beginning to open, some deep breathing or yawning, and some turning or stretching on the bed. All the physical senses begin to awaken too.

As the new day's demands begin to speak, and the natural functions begin to get the message, natural thinking begins to be required. We saw earlier that natural thoughts tend to quench dream-thoughts at this point because they may offend the conscious character of the individual. So a good idea, obviously, is to wake up slowly.

As soon as you realize you have awakened, determine not to open your eyes, move around, or stretch your body. Don't talk to anyone or fuss with the alarm clock or radio. Being awakened abruptly by a person or alarm clock can cause dream-thoughts which were being disclosed to become closed up again in your subconscious mind very quickly. So quickly can this happen, in fact, that you may not even realize that you have dreamed a significant dream. Any alarming activity can do this easily, so they should be avoided if possible. Your waking up experience should not be an alarming one.

It may be helpful to prayerfully and effortfully practise waking up without any alarms. In my experience, I find that when I need to be up at a certain time, and ask God to wake me up by then, he usually gets me up about ten to twenty minutes earlier, and I feel fine. I have also found earplugs to be helpful because I live in a busy neighbour-hood and often sleep during the day. It disturbs me when my dreams are interrupted unnecessarily because I hear from God in dreams constantly. It is for my need to be able to recall my dreams that I have, through much prayer and study, discovered these practical principles.

While waking up, first try to be still for awhile and mind your dreams. If possible, don't even take a deep breath right away--not yet. The more you perceive and yield to the demands of the day before you, the more they will call you. But by ignoring those demands for a few moments, while the door is still open between consciousness and subconsciousness, dream-thoughts which may help you somehow--which are getting ready to slip away--can be arrested and brought into full consciousness.

When you are satisfied that you have remembered enough dream-thoughts, and that their meaning is within your reach, then you can open your eyes, take a deep breath, and stretch out. Then you can commence to interpret the dream. Or you can work on the interpreting as soon as you recall the dream before getting completely up.

What can happen here, however, is that you will slip back into sleep. The body isn't fully awake yet, only the mind is. And since you are meditating on dreams, it is easy to slip back into that realm and dream some more. Then when you wake up again later, you might not recall at all what you began to recall earlier. This has happened to me many times.

When they are supernatural, actual, angelic, or trance-like dreams (as these terms are defined in Chapter 8), there will be less of a problem in recalling or interpreting the messages of God because they are then most impactful.

But the natural dreams usually require natural effort to work with, even though they may contain messages from God. Remember, God may speak to us in supernatural dreams, and also in natural dreams.

Ask God for remembrance, even plead with Him for awhile if necessary. Jesus said, "Ask, and it shall be given you," (Matthew 7:7). Yet it isn't always given to us immediately. At times, we must knock and keep on knocking on Jesus' door, that by our continual coming--yes, our importunity--we might receive our request, (Luke 11:8).

I awaken knowing that I just had a dream, and somehow I'm sure it was of God. There is something useful in it from which I can gain if only I can remember it. I can pray:

"Lord, You know I'm seeking Your will, and I need some answers. I think this dream will help me. Please, Lord, please give me remembrance. I ask You in Jesus' Name, please help me remember this dream so that I can see Your will more clearly, because I intend to walk in it obediently, for Your glory. In Jesus' Name. Amen."

This asking may take a little while. But if God is pleased to reveal it, He will. Now some people might argue, "We shouldn't bother God too much. Leave well enough alone. Don't inquire into such fickle things as dreams. If God would speak to you in a dream, you would remember it regardless of your prayers and efforts or lack thereof. If you don't remember it, it is because He doesn't want you to know it."

It is true that God does not want us to know all our dreams, and He doesn't speak in all our dreams. Therefore, we should draw the line where He does and not be too quick to pray such prayers. However, when a person is convinced that a dream of his came from God, and that it contains insights which he can benefit from, who can blame him for seeking those goodly pearls and trading his prayers for them?

As we delight ourselves in the Lord, He gives us the desires of our hearts, (Psalms 37:4). When we are committed to the Lord, our desires are inspired of Him. But we must prayerfully express those desires unto Him in order that the Holy Spirit may respond to us again. If He doesn't interrupt or discourage our asking to recall a dream, it is likely He will give us remembrance of it.

Proverbs 2:3-5 Yea, if thou criest after knowledge, and liftest up thy voice for understanding; If thou seekest her as silver, and searchest for her as for hid treasures; Then shalt thou understand the fear of the Lord, and find the knowledge of God.

Jeremiah 29:12-13 Then shall ye call upon Me, and go and pray unto Me, and I will hearken unto you. And ye shall seek Me, and find Me, when ye shall search for Me with all your heart.

Dream Interpretation

God speaks to us in dreams more often than we realize. Sometimes His messages are clearly supernatural, as with Daniel the Prophet, and with Joseph the Dreamer. But most of the time, dreams with messages from the Lord are not so spectacular. They can be very similar to regular dreams, yet they do provide wisdoms from on high.

Sometimes God's message in a dream is easily under-stood. It may have no symbols, no indistinct images or sounds, and may be immediately and fully recalled. Such dreams leave little or no room for misinterpretation and help us move confidently in that which has been revealed. But most dreams contain at least one or more symbols for which we must work at interpreting.

We can first recall and interpret the symbols in a dream in order to understand the message. Herein we are using the knowledge we have about symbols to understand God's message. Or we can, through prayer, first get "a sense" of what God is saying (what mood He's in, where He's coming from, by what spirit He's speaking, and who or what He's generally referring to), then we'll know how to acknowledge and interpret the symbols. Getting a sense of the message first, helps us in understanding the symbols.

One way to begin getting a sense of what God is saying in a dream is to first determine His expression or His approach. Is the message something He's smiling upon, or something He's frowning at? At times I have perceived a pleasant presence from the Lord in dreams, and at other times a joyous presence. I have also perceived a loving presence, a concerned presence, a discontented presence, and even a presence that has made me literally quake in my bed. The "quaking" can be a scolding, a statement of His power, a healing, a revelation of an imminent earthquake, or maybe something else.

Another question you may begin asking the Lord is, "For whom is the message intended?" Does it seem to point directly to you? Or does it seem to point to someone else? Or, if there's a broad sense to it, does it seem to concern a certain body of people? Another possibility is that if the sense of a dream inspires you to hope, it may concern the future, for the future gives us hope.

Interestingly, dreams about the future may involve symbols which you will only understand sometime in the future. A Christian I know dreamed of a palm tree, and had no idea of what it meant. She told two of her friends, young ministers who had been looking for a place to start a Church (as God had instructed them). When they found a storefront place for rent, they saw a sign above the entrance with a drawing of a palm tree. This was a confirmation to them that God wanted them there. And after they began services, God glorified Himself there in some marvelous ways, confirming the dream with signs and wonders following. See how the palm tree was only understood sometime after the dream occurred, after other events fell into place?

Most symbols can be interpreted in different ways, depending upon the message. Much symbolism is used in dreams because God is a Spirit (John 4:24) and His messages must "fall down" into the natural realm, our minds and lives. We must relate the revelations of His

Spirit to things in the natural realm as the natural things are understood by us personally, by collective groups, or universally by men as a whole. And in a given dream, some symbols may be understood by us, and other symbols by a collective body.

Interpretations of symbols, as a rule, will be according to what is familiar to us. That's why "personal" symbols differ greatly between individuals but "collective" or "universal" symbols do not. And the meaning of a symbol can be found in the knowledge we already have. This is why we should familiarize ourselves with the meanings of symbols according to the Bible. If I haven't learned that a sword symbolizes the Word of God, I probably won't receive that symbol in message about the Word of God. And if I do, I might not "get the message."

Dreams with messages for the general public contain symbols (when they do) that have more or less universal applications. You may immediately begin to interpret them as public messages when they involve such symbols. Biblically, oil represents the anointing of God's Holy Spirit Who indwells the collective Body of Christ. Therefore, in a dream with the symbol of oil, we may immediately begin to understand it as a message applicable to all Christians. Of course, there are exceptions.

A dream with symbols which pertain to you specifically as an individual is a message intended for you. In beginning to interpret it, you may immediately understand that it's not for someone who doesn't relate to those symbols. If I like turtleneck sweaters, I know that item symbolizes me in a dream, especially if I don't know anyone else who likes them. If I know a person who wears wide ties, he may be symbolized in my dream by a wide tie. The message in that dream will not apply to someone else because that symbol doesn't.

A dream may come forth as a moving scenario (or a few of them) or as a still picture (or a few of them). In one scenario or in one picture, a person might see many details. A picture paints a thousand words. And a dream, even if it's only one picture, can include many details, each with its own message.

I may dream of driving a car. The kind of car it is, if that's a prominent detail, may mean a specific thing to me. What kind of road I'm travelling on, if that's a prominent detail, may mean something specific to me also. What color shirt I'm wearing, how I'm feeling, who's with me in the car, and other details may each speak a particular point if they stand out somehow. The overall message is what I'm really looking for, but the more details which I can identify and interpret, the more of the mind of Christ will I have.

I dreamed I was conversing with several Christians. One of them, a medical doctor, was attending to a woman with a lower back problem, and the words "LOWER LUMBAR" were shown in capital letters over that part of her body. The main message from God to me in this dream had nothing at all to do with "lower lumbar," and in reality I had never heard that term before. But the fact that it is a term actually used in medical science (I checked it out afterward to "test" this particular detail) lends support to the validity of the whole dream. This also shows us that we can learn new things in dreams which we have never studied before.

If that term was not verifiable, if it really applied to something else, I might have questioned the validity of the other details. This is where we have to learn how to distinguish and separate between the wheat and the chaff in dreams, as we studied in Chapter 4. However, when all the details in a dream are factual, consistent, and flow together like clockwork, it's easier to see God in it, as we shall see in Chapter 6.

A certain dream from God may seem to contradict another dream from God, as also occurs with prophecies, words of wisdom, and other revelations from Him. Such differences are simply varied portions of the mind of Christ. We may or may not understand the full meanings of the various messages they disclose, but they may still be of Him. However they may come, God's messages often seem to contradict each other, but in reality He never contradicts Himself.

I've received differing leadings from the Lord in dreams. I would see myself go forth preaching and ministering, and soon afterward I would see myself meditating, staying still before God, and waiting upon Him. I would ask, "Lord, what should I do, go forth or stay? I don't understand." He told me that they were all valid ideas, even the seeming contradictions. In certain matters He wanted me to go forth, in certain other matters He wanted me to be still in His presence and wait on Him. Those certain matters were clarified after prayer, interestingly enough, partly through more dreams.

I've dreamed of a great Holy Ghost revival coming to America, as many other Christians have. I've also dreamed of great crises coming in our economy, government, religious life, and in other areas, as many others have dreamed. As Christians may prophesy of great blessings coming, and also of great judgments coming, we may also dream of these because both prophecies and dreams are channels through which God speaks and makes known the things that He will do. Such revelations from God are addressing different matters but they're not contradicting one another (if indeed they are inspired of Him).

We should broaden our capacity for a biblical under-standing of the move of God in the last days. Then we can tolerate what might at first appear to be contradicting revelations. When we deduce that a couple of revelations are clearly irreconcilable, then clearly they're not all from God, for He is not the author of division and confusion, (Matthew 12:25; 1Corinthians 14:33).

For a person to interpret another persons dream, he should consider the dreamer's understanding of the sym-bols and how they relate to him personally. This is especially true when the symbols are not universal or scripturally-based ones. Special care, wisdom, patience, and prayer, should be exercised when endeavouring to help others understand their dreams. We should decline from, or be quick to drop if necessary, dream interpreting when we're not both knowledgeable and anointed in this area. People want to be helped, but it's very easy to do more harm than good in the name of spiritual counsel and spiritual gifts.

Dreams with messages from God are not overly complicated. He talks our language, even though with symbols. He'll talk to you in your own language--relate to you personally as you would understand Him--even though with symbols. If we do our part to understand His message, we should be able to interpret and get the message. It's only when we're having trouble grasping the interpretation of a dream or vision that we should consult some of the pointers here.

God has given us a biblical code, we might say, by which we can define symbols. As we mature in our understanding of His Word, He will use His symbols more often, as they are used in the Bible. His messages will be clearer and more divine unto us when we can understand His efficacious symbols instead of the lower, more personal ones we learn naturally. When He is forced to speak to us by the symbols we understand naturally, we might discard His dreams as we do natural ones.

Now one might say, "Yes, but, we don't have to go through all of that to figure out in our minds what God is trying to say. If God gives us a dream, He will get His message across, He will interpret it. After all, you know, the Bible does say, 'Interpretations belong to God.'"

Yes, this is our underlying, indisputable understanding, "Interpretations belong to God," (Genesis 40:8; Daniel 2:28). However, He wants us to be about trading and doing business with the talents He has given us. We should exercise our souls in spiritual knowledge by faith.

If all His messages, through dreams and otherwise, were unmistakably clear, we would have no choice about it but to walk by the *sight* He would give us. But when we interpret His messages by faith in the tools His Word provides us, we can please Him, because we're believing and obeying His message *by faith,* and not by having seen an unmistakable vision. And, of course, He communicates to us on our level of faith and of knowledge. Yet He wants us to always be growing in both.

In one dream from the Holy Spirit which I had, I was having difficulty with the interpretation. I asked Jesus, "Why don't You just give me the meaning clearly? Why all the symbolism? Why do You use these 'parables of the eye' and not speak plainly?" He answered, "I want you to learn how to use your mind and the knowledge you've gained, and stretch it." I rejoiced to hear His voice, and gladly proceeded to enucleate, expose His message. Praise the Lord! At times, though, He provides the interpretation supernaturally, beyond our natural comprehension, reminding us of our complete dependency upon Him. We're never going to ascend our minds above His. Amen.

Sometimes you could figure out the meaning of a dream by the knowledge you already have in your mind. When a Midianite soldier dreamed a symbolic dream (Judges 7:13-14), his fellow soldier, who was neither a dreamer nor a diviner, immediately interpreted it. He understood the symbol of "barley bread" to represent Gideon, who was a barley thresher.

When Joseph the Dreamer dreamed of his brethren bowing down to him in reverence, and told it to them, they immediately understood its meaning, though it involved symbols. When he dreamed of his parents and brethren together bowing down to him in reverence, and told it to his father Jacob, his father immediately understood its prophetical meaning, though it involved symbols too, (Genesis 37:5-11).

At first a dream may puzzle us. But after interpreting it, we may respond, "Oh yes, of course, what else could it mean? Now that I understand it, I realize no other meaning is possible." Remember, God talks our language, even though with symbols. He won't give us a completely "uncertain sound," for then we'll not know what is being spoken, (1Corinthians 14:7-11).

Pharaoh's supernatural dream was not necessarily difficult to interpret (Genesis 41:25). When Joseph was called upon to interpret the Pharaoh's dream, he didn't pray to God--he was already "prayed-up." He immediately and unhesitatingly gave the full interpretation as soon as the dream was told him. He even proceeded to counsel the king and advise what he should do.

Nebuchadnezzar's supernatural dream was not necessarily difficult to interpret either, (Daniel 4:27). When Daniel was called upon to interpret the king's dream, he didn't pray to God--he was already "prayed-up" also. He immediately, within the hour, gave the full interpretation when it was told him. Only he was troubled for a few minutes because of the profundity of the revelation. Daniel also proceeded to counsel his king and advise what he should do in response to God's message.

Yes, interpretations belong to God, and He gave to Joseph and to Daniel understanding in the interpretation of dreams. Yes, you should pray to the Lord for help in accurately interpreting His messages. But when a message is presented to you and you are able to decipher it with the knowledge you already have, and the Holy Spirit "bears witness" with it, God has thereby revealed the interpretation whether or not you have prayed about it in a formal way. When God answers our need, He first inquires at His storehouse in us, and feeds us therefrom. For this reason He commands us:

2Timothy 2:15 Study to shew thyself approved unto God, a workman that needeth not to be ashamed, rightly dividing the Word of Truth.

Now ancient heathen nations such as Babylon and Egypt had schools of knowledge. Their magicians, diviners, soothsayers, and sorcerers diligently studied the arts, sciences, and other disciplines of their times. These "wise men" (falsely so-called) were learned in witchcraft, sorcery, magic, divination, astrology, mathematics, medicine, linguistics, philosophy, psychology, dreams, visions, and in other fields of knowledge.

In their schools, these things were taught and practised. When consulted, these men would use the understanding they had and would produce solutions to problems. They would use medicines for healing, mathematics in business matters, foreign languages for communicating with other nations, and so on.

When it came to spiritual matters, these men would employ demonic spirits to assist them. They were often able to interpret visions, dreams, and other extranatural phenomena, through their knowledge in these areas, and by the aid of spiritual forces. We must understand that they enjoyed a fair degree of accuracy. Otherwise they would never be consulted, much less organize schools.

No doubt the prosperity and conquests which many ancient civilizations enjoyed were largely due to the insights, predictions, and maneuvers which their diviners advised their kings and captains. No wonder that diviners held significant positions in governments and were highly esteemed as the elite.

Many of God's servants throughout the centuries (such as the Patriarch Moses, and the Prophet Daniel) were learned in all of the knowledge and skills of the heathen nations in which they lived. Why did God allow or cause this to be so? All religions contain some true, sound principles of life which can be used for practical purposes. God wanted some of His servants to learn some things in order to improve their manner of conversation among the Gentiles, and gain an audience with them. However, God removed them from these schools before they got to practise their skills in league with wicked spirits.

Moses became mighty in words and in deeds in Egypt, (Acts 7:22). Yet we may suppose he never worked the works of the Egyptian magicians, his peers, before he left Egypt and had his "burning bush" experience with the Lord.

While in captivity, Daniel and his brethren became ten

times better than all of Babylon's magicians and astrologers in all matters of wisdom and understanding that their king inquired of them, including in all aspects of visions and dreams, (Daniel 1:7). Had God approved of idolatry and witchcraft? No. God gave the Hebrews His own knowledge pertaining to their studies, while their fellow students and teachers worshipped false gods.

God gave them His knowledge because they had purposed in their hearts not to defile themselves with the heathen diet and, as well, with the heathen practises. Thus He indicted the heathen nations for following other gods and censured their witchcrafts. The heathen nations did not worship the true and living God. In all of their devilish doctrines and idolatrous worship, they never raised a standard of holiness and reverence to Jehovah.

Daniel and his fellow Hebrews studied in the heathen schools, but God didn't endorse the heathenistic teachings. Every time they're mentioned in the Bible, it's with disdain. God would've allowed all of Babylon's so-called wise men to perish were it not for the prayers of Daniel and his three Hebrew brethren, (Daniel 2:16-18).

We can study various academic fields, but we should also purpose that we will not defile ourselves with doctrines of devils. We can be in the world, but not of it. It is not uncommon to find a Christian led by God to study in a secular institution. In many schools, their are many curricula which God doesn't endorse. Yet He may lead some of His people through them so that they may become wise in secular knowledge. This way, they can gain an audience among those who are in the world without ever compromising their faith in Christ. We can observe, analyze, and weigh things as we gain knowledge, all the while touching not the unclean things.

All truth comes from God. In this natural world, the universal laws and principles which the Lord created are systematizeable and practicable, able to be enforced for our own purposes. And since our purpose is to serve God in spirit and in truth, we should acknowledge and consult

His scriptural symbol-language when interpreting His messages.

Also important is the fact that a person's culture and upbringing partly influence his perception and understanding of symbols. Military strength might today be symbolized by nuclear missiles and tanks, instead of the older (yet still scriptural) symbols of horses and chariots. Worship unto the Lord might today be symbolized by a guitar, instead of the scriptural symbol of a harp. Therefore, to a degree, symbols may come and go with eras, dispensations, or customs.

Now some symbols may be of private interpretation. Transportation may be symbolized as a bicycle to one group, while it may be shown as an automobile to another. More private still may be the symbol of a desk. To one person, it may mean studying, to another it may mean office work, and to still another it may mean a promotion at their workplace.

In order to interpret the revelations which God gives us in dreams and visions, we can open up our understanding with some questions. A good habit would be to ask ourselves: "What does this symbol mean in the Bible? What does this symbol mean today, or in my culture? What does this symbol mean to the person the dream is about? What does this symbol mean personally to me?"

Some symbols in a dream are more than just images used to represent messages. They can be pictures of literal items. For example, a desk might mean more than just that I should study more. It might mean that God wants me to buy a desk, or that I'm going to receive one somehow so that I can study more. Or it may have a great number of other possible meanings.

When an image is to be taken literally, but we're not sure about it yet, the best thing to do is pray for clarity or confirmation, and wait on God. When messages are to be understood or acted upon literally, an assurance will come in some familiar form. God will never require too much from us without giving us enough to go on.

The following classification includes some very common and basic symbols. Some of these are very broad generalizations and allow for many exceptions, particularly when they are found in personal messages. Interpreting these symbols correctly depends, more often than not, on several variables, such as: other symbols within the message, what they mean to the person who received it, his emotional disposition, and most of all, his personal situation at the time he received it.

Symbols Common in Dreams and Visions

1) Numbers

God's use of numbers in the Bible is always premeditated. Also in dreams and visions inspired by Him, we may find significant messages in the numbers used. Sometimes the numbers are to be understood literally, at times symbolically.

In dreams and visions, as in real life, numbers may be involved with only a general meaning, without having a specific significance. A number found in a dream or vision does not always have a profound message from the Lord for us. The more supernatural the revelation is, the more significant will the numbers be. What a certain number represents in the Scriptures, it may also represent in dreams and visions. And numbers in the Bible generally represent either good things or evil things, (positive or negative, favourable or unfavourable, yes or no).

Basically, the number one (1) means God, principal part, beginning, or good; two (2) means witness, agreement, division, or evil; three (3) means trinity--Father, Son, and Holy Ghost, or completeness; four (4) means wholeness, such as that of the world--north, south, east, and west; five (5) means grace; six (6) means man; seven (7) means Jesus Christ, or complete perfection; eight (8) means new beginning; nine (9) means fullness, or end; ten (10) means governmental order, or totality; eleven (11) means incompleteness; twelve (12) means divine order; thirteen (13) means rebellion; thirty (30) means separation and readiness; forty (40) means testing and trial; fifty (50) means Pentecost, rejoicing, revival, and restoration.

When a number is given in hundreds, thousands, millions, or in any multiplied form (such as 700, 12,000, or 50,000,000, etc.), it has the same meaning as the first character, only then with multiplied intensity. Unless, of course, the figure given is intended to be taken literally and not symbolically.

2) Colors

When a color is outstanding, as though emphasis is being given to it, the meaning of that color should help in the interpretation. Generally, white means pure, clean, righteous, or God; black means death, evil, or Satan (the prince of darkness); red means blood, violence, or fervent (fired-up for God, or fired-up for the devil); green means life, growth, or prosperity; blue means peace, or heavenly; purple means royal, or kingly; silver means strength, or redemption; gold means divine, precious, or pure; the rainbow means promise or covenant, and serves to remind us of God's promises. The rainbow is a very good symbol in dreams and visions because it encourages us to praise God and trust that He will do what He said He will do.

3) Animals

Fish means people as a harvest of souls for Jesus; sheep means Christians; dove means Holy Spirit; a horse means strength; depending upon what God is saying, a lion can represent Jesus Christ, the saints of God, or Satan; evil spirits (either demons, or sinful humans) can be symbolized by serpents, scorpions, dogs, bugs, other unclean animals, or evil human beings. Animals may also represent nations, and they may be shown in a positive light, or in a negative light.

4) Things

A tree means a person, king, or nation; precious stones means saints, those who are precious to God; a star means an angel, a special person, or a special mark of achievement and honour; a key means authority, right-of-way, or the power and opportunity to open a door; a door means an opportunity; a gun means power; a spot means a sin or sinner; a toilet or toilet paper means there is a need for deliverance (purging); a cross means Christianity, or picking up your cross to follow Jesus; money may mean provision, prosperity, or the means by which one may prosper financially or in some other way.

5) False Religions

These are most often symbolized by incense, candles, statues, carved stones, strange images, ancient figures, ancient temples, and other non-Christian things.

6) Directions

Right means favour; left means disfavour; right hand means strength; left hand means weakness; up or high means spiritual, or heavenly-minded; down or low means natural, or carnally-minded; distant and dim images or sounds may mean not in the near future; near and clear images or sounds may mean soon or very soon.

7) Actions

Activity may mean industriousness; stillness may mean dormancy; running may mean fervency, or urgency; flying may mean freedom, or liberty; falling may mean regression, or defeat, losing control of circumstances, or being lost spiritually; yelling, vomiting, or excessive coughing may mean deliverance from evil spirits, because when people are being delivered from them, they may experience those things; defecation and urination may also mean deliverance, a purging of unnecessary things; eating or drinking may mean satisfaction, provision, indulgence, overindulgence, or communion and fellowship (if eating with others). Many great biblical events occurred around a meal, such as the Last Supper of our Lord.

Standing may mean being ready; walking may mean progress; sitting may mean the work is done; smiling may mean approval; frowning may mean disapproval; laughing may mean gladness; crying may mean suffering; kissing may mean blessing, friendship, relationship, or intimacy (again, all depending on other variables within the context of the message).

Sexual activity in dreams can mean a great many things, and can also be interpreted either literally or symbolically. Among the possible meanings are: a future encounter (if it's a warning through a *word of wisdom*), or a secret desire on your part or the other person's (if it's a *discerning of spirits*), or maybe something else. These revelations may be inspired by God for our understanding. A sexual dream may also speak of intimate communion, a need to be accepted, a need to express sensuality, a memory, or lust. These may be caused by the natural mind and heart, or by the devil, or by both.

8)   Nations

Dreams from the Lord are always important. They are usually given to mature, serious Christians, and are clearly expressed. When they appear with symbols, the symbols may be the nation's flag, currency, topographical features, national monuments, other distinct details, or any combination of these. The Great Wall means China; the Eiffle Tower means France; the Great Pyramids means Egypt; Mount Fuji means Japan; the Dome of the Rock or the Wailing Wall means Israel; the Statue of Liberty means America.

Likewise cities and states may be symbolized by distinct

features, buildings, or monuments. The White House may represent Washington, D.C.; the Grand Canyon, Arizona; Diamond Head, Hawaii; the Empire State Building, New York City.

Ramon Moran, a friend of mine and missionary to Venezuela, South America, had made several attempts to visit New York City one summer. But he was repeatedly hindered. After much prayer, the Lord showed him a vision of the skyline of Manhattan (New York City), and snow was falling. He then knew that God wanted him to visit in the winter time, which he was able to do. And God used him mightily there in confirmation of His Word.

9) Persons

A baby means a new Christian, or immaturity; a child means a young Christian; a lady or bride means the Body of Christ, the Church of God; a lady may also represent a country; a leper means a sinner; weeds means sinners; wheat or wheatfields means saints; masses of peoples may be symbolized by waters, by trees, or by flocks of cattle.

In spiritual dreams, and also in natural dreams, an individual may symbolically represent another person. I have a natural brother, Charlie, who is one year older than me. I have often seen him in dreams, usually representing himself. But at times he has symbolically represented a certain close friend of mine, Isaac, who is also a brother in the Lord. Charlie has also represented Jesus Christ in a couple of my dreams when He wanted to relate to me as an older brother. Jesus Christ is as an Elder Brother to all Christians, and at the same time, a Friend that sticks closer than a brother, (Proverbs 18:24).

In a dream from the Lord, I was preaching and a young black girl stood directly before me understanding and believing everything I spoke. She may have symbolized black Christians who are spiritually young, babes in Christ, and the dream may have been showing me that God was planning to send me unto them. Or it may have meant that I was going to meet that particular person sometime in the future, if she was to be understood literally.

Therefore, at times, I must first get a sense of what God is saying before interpreting the symbols. Then I'll know just how to interpret them, and I'll know whether to acknowledge them symbolically or literally. Other details in the dream may assist me in getting a sense of the message. Or if the interpretation doesn't come forth, I can simply commit it back unto the Lord and see what His providence unfolds in my life.

10)   Jesus Christ

He's often symbolized as a Shepherd, Priest, King, Lord, Brother, Friend, Mountain, Rock, Ark, Fortress, Sword, Sun, or Flower (the Rose of Sharon or Lily of the Valley).

11)   The Holy Ghost

He is often symbolized as oil, wine, wind, fire (such as cloven tongues of fire); or by some form of water (such as rain, vapour, a flood, a wave, a river, or a well). The Holy Spirit may also be symbolized as a lady, because one of His anointings (presences) is gentle comfort, as that of a lady.

12)   God's Word

The Word of God is symbolized as a seed, corn, bread, meat, a lamp, a hammer, a sickle, a sword, or a Bible.

Diversities of Impressions

In addition to interpreting symbols, dreams can also be understood through impressions, feelings, or words. The impression or feeling you have about a certain dream may help you determine its meaning. It may be the key to the meaning.

You may have a friend who is about to get married, and in the visible, natural realm of circumstance everything seems fine. In a dream, you may see the ceremony taking place and everything there seems fine. When you awaken you may have a feeling of uneasiness, though you might not understand why. The Holy Ghost might thereby be sharing His feeling on that matter with you, perhaps so that you'll sound an alarm against that marriage.

A dream may consist of words with no images. While sleeping once, I simply heard the Lord say, "James has found his wife." My friend James, whom I hadn't seen for several months, was single when I last saw or heard from him. When I heard this message from the Spirit, I didn't know if it meant that he had gotten married, or that he had found the lady whom he was going to marry. Soon afterward, I saw James and found the latter to be the case. And still they are happily married and have two children. Praise God.

In a dream, the presence of someone you know may be felt, though you don't see or hear them. You may possibly at this time discern what spirit they're of, or what spirit they're in.

A dream may be interpreted in the process of time as one's life progresses. Peter's vision of the grafting in of the Gentiles was explained to him by the next day's providence. When Cornelius and other non-Jews were born-again and filled with the mighty Holy Ghost and spoke in other tongues and magnified God, then Peter understood that God's message of salvation was to be preached in all the world, to every creature (Jew *and* Gentile). Whereas at first Peter had doubted in himself what this vision of all kinds of unclean animals which he had seen should mean, (Acts 10).

A message from the Holy Spirit may show you things to come (the future) in a way you can't relate to now. But as your life progresses and God unfolds His will in your life, then you can understand what God had revealed to you in that dream.

Joseph the Dreamer at first didn't understand the gravity of his dreams of being exalted above his brethren. Perhaps while in prison he encouraged himself in the Lord and recalled those dreams of earlier years. By meditating on them, he may have caused himself to dream similar dreams, thereby keeping the "dream" alive. He found strong consolation as he laid hold upon the hope set before him. He had a vision, a goal, and therefore prospered while in prison until the time that God's message to him came to pass. He endured all of this without knowing how or when the vision would come to pass.

Why would God leave us with an unclear message? Shouldn't He clarify His plan or not speak it at all? He may want you to catch enough of a glimpse of His will so that you'll yield enough to it, but not too much that you'll get in His way and hinder it from being fulfilled. That's why after working on the interpretation of a given dream, if you have not understood the whole of it, you should commit it back unto the Lord. If He feels you should understand it more, He will give it again, perhaps in another way--if not, He won't. In either case, I advise as King Nebuchadnezzar advised the Prophet Daniel, "Let not dreams or their interpretations trouble you," (Daniel 4:19 author's paraphrase).

Chapter 6

Try the Dreams
Whether they are of God

1 John 4:1 Beloved, believe not every spirit,
but try the spirits whether they are of God.

The United States Treasury Department is skilled in distinguishing genuine currencies from counterfeit. Interestingly, Treasury experts do not major in examining the counterfeit coins and bills--this would take too long. They major in examining genuine monies, learning what real money is like--how it feels, what it reads, its color, paper quality, and other properties. Then when they come across a counterfeit, they know it is fake because it lacks those qualities which real money has.

And so it is with the things of God, including dreams. We don't have to study a lot about ungodly dreams and their workings so that we can identify them when we come across them. We have got to know God's Word according to sound doctrine, study the scriptural significance of dreams, become familiar with the ways of the Holy Spirit, seek to know Him more and more each day, and associate ourselves closely with those who are truly anointed of Him. Then if we have a dream with a spirit (or a "sense") other than that which we have received, we know it is not of God (Galatians 1:8-9), even though we may not understand in great detail what it is all about.

Now if a certain currency is made obsolete, counterfeiters wouldn't try to copy it. Right? But they only try to copy that which is still valid. And so it is with prophecies, visions, dreams, gifts of the Holy Ghost, and other supernatural manifestations, as well as with the written Word of God. The only reason why there are ungodly manifestations is because there are godly ones. If there weren't any from God, the devil wouldn't have anything to copy. But we don't throw away all of our money just because there are some counterfeit dollars going around. We find the true and work with it!

Now one might say, "But all those supernatural things are only as chaff compared to wheat. All we need is the written Word of God, which is the more sure word of prophecy," (2Peter 1:19). But the Bible doesn't say that all supernatural manifestations are as chaff compared to God's Word. The Bible says that only the false ones are as chaff compared to wheat, God's Word. The dreams which are truly of God are God's Word in manifestation. Dreams from God and the written Word of God are all as wheat. Whereas those which are not inspired of Him are as chaff (tares, weeds).

The Apostle Paul said that he preached in demonstration of the Spirit and of power, so that our faith should stand in that power, (1Corinthians 2:4-5). Elihu too, one of Job's friends, believed that God demonstrated Himself in dreams, (Job 33:14-16). He had enjoyed neither the Holy Bible nor the baptism in the Holy Ghost with fire. In addition, he lived generations before God began disclosing supernatural revelations in dreams and visions unto His servants Abraham, Moses, and the canonized prophets. Yet Elihu plainly acknowledged dreams and visions as being a major avenue through which God often speaks to men. Dreams have always been used by God (and also by other spirits) as an avenue to speak to men, and men have always known this.

The letter of God's Word by itself kills (enhances our sinfulness and our separation from God), but the Spirit of God's Word gives life when He is manifested, (2Corinthians 3:6). All supernatural demonstrations inspired by God are God's Word in manifestation, and as such they are foundations for our faith. God's people will prosper, in spiritual ways and in natural ways, as we base our faith in God's Word--whether it is revealed in simple ways, or in super ways.

Paul's ministry prospered because he was not disobedient but had faith in the heavenly visions shown him, (Acts 26:19). He believed God's Word, not as it was taught to him by man, but by the revelations of Jesus Christ, (Galatians 1:12). His faith was founded on God's Word disclosed supernaturally.

Faith comes by hearing, and hearing by the Word of God (the *rhema* of God). His rhema, the current living message His Spirit is speaking unto us at a particular time, may come in a dream or vision. Therefore, we can stand on it because it is His manifested Word, His Word as it is intended for us personally.

Remember, much of the written Word of God came via dreams and visions, and about a third of the Bible context involves them. So the same Spirit which authored the Word in the past can presently make alive the portions we require--again via dreams and visions. All supernatural revelations inspired by God excite faith and can be foundations for our faith.

Jeremiah 23:28-29 The prophet that hath a dream, let him tell a dream; and he that hath My Word, let him speak My Word faithfully. What is the chaff to the wheat? saith the Lord. Is not My Word like as a fire? saith the Lord; and like a hammer that breaketh the rock in pieces?

In the context of Jeremiah 23, God is reprimanding false prophets. However, He is also indicating, "My Word is like a fire, it'll sanctify, heal, and revive. My Word is like a hammer that will break fetters, destroy yokes, pull down strongholds, and level mountains. My Word is like wheat, nourishment, in comparison to chaff, worthless material. So let the prophet prophesy, let the dreamer dream. If it's of Me, it'll bring life--if it's not, it won't.

1Thessalonians 5:19-21 Quench not the Spirit. Despise not prophesyings. Prove all things; hold fast that which is good.

1Thessalonians 5:19-21 (niv) Do not put out the Spirit's fire; do not treat prophecies with contempt. Test everything. Hold on to the good.

1Thessalonians 5:19-21 (tev) Do not restrain the Holy Spirit; do not despise inspired messages. Put all things to the test: keep what is good.

Clear enough? Don't limit God. Don't hinder God. Don't grieve God. Don't despise or reject the messages He inspires, howsoever they may come. As verse 20 says (in the King James Version) "Despise not prophesyings," we can also say, "Despise not dreamings." Because in the Bible, and still today, prophetic messages often come through dreams.

Let the Spirit flow. Embrace the demonstration of the Spirit with power. Despise not dreams and visions. Try (test) the spirits behind dreams and see whether they are of God, knowing that your spirit will hold firmly to that which is good. You'll bear witness with that which is of God.

As a rule, the more profound dreams from God are experienced in the Body of Christ by apostles, prophets, and intercessors. They're right next to Jesus Christ, the Chief Cornerstone of God's building, the Head of the Church, the Revealer, (Ephesians 2:20; 4:11-12; 1Corinthians 12:28; Revelation 21:14; and Jeremiah 9:17-20).

A new Christian can and often does receive a message from God in a dream, supernaturally and otherwise. But messages which have universal applications to the Body of Christ, or which have major political significance, or which can affect the entire course of a person's life or ministry, these and others of this weight are given through the foundational ministries. This is why Christians should share their revelations with God's anointed servants. This way they will be judged and acknowledged in the right spirit.

Likewise when a prophet receives a profound message from God, he also should share it with fellow apostles and prophets. This way all are edified and illuminated concerning God's work, and the Holy Spirit can bring confirmation, and possibly further revelation, through that company.

Obviously, though, we should not share our dreams casually, carelessly, or prematurely. Joseph did so and got himself into trouble as a result, (Genesis 37:5-11). The Midianite soldier also foolishly shared his dream and thereby caused the complete defeat of his army, (Judges 7:13-14). For having been too quick to declare a dream from the Lord, many Christians have spoken words out of season and caused unnecessary setbacks and friction within the Church.

There is a belief among Middle Eastern cultures, that a dream or vision loses its initial power when it is first spoken. If this is true, then I can see why God often tells us not to share a revelation He has given us, at least not immediately. It may be that an inspired dream is planted in us as a seed and needs time to grow if it is going to produce fruit.

When the time is right and the message is ripe, then we can translate into a *prophetic word of the Lord* the dream inspired by the Lord. The person whom the message is for has been made ready, our own spirit has carried it full-term, and the spiritual impact is greatest then. Premature delivery of a message from the Lord can hinder the work of God and cause problems. When we ask the Lord what to do with our dreams--when to speak them and when to wait--we avoid many problems.

When we do share a revelation from the Lord, our level of credibility with that individual or group will figure in the level and amount of revelation we share. Indeed, the latter should not exceed the former unless the Lord Himself opens the doors of people's hearts and gives us special favour with them. Unless the Lord supernaturally ignites us, we should not insist on gaining an audience for our revelations--that's the quickest way to lose credibility.

When we have gained credibility in the Body of Christ through servant-heartedness and faithfulness in ordinary duties, then it is more likely that our prophetic/revelatory giftings will be acknowledged and received with optimal effect. You may care for someone's children for a year or two, or pass the offering plate in Church for some time, or humble yourself under the mighty hand of God in some other way, before the Lord exalts you for His glory and finally releases you to share your revelatory insights. And, so that we may be honourable vessels approved by God when that time comes, it behooves us to be prayerful and studious until then.

The Bible clearly establishes that anything which contradicts God's Word is erroneous, howsoever supernatural or spectacular it may be. We must stand firmly upon sound teaching as we incline to dreams, visions, and revelations of the Lord. We can most fully yield to supernatural experiences and to spiritual revelations when we know God's Word, the Rock wherein we trust.

Many dreams, by themselves, are very profound and symbolic, and might seem to have no biblical support. Therefore, we must "catch the spirit" of the message so that we can receive the dream in the proper spirit.

When the Apostle Peter experienced a trance, he received an extraordinary vision with a new revelation from God, (Acts 10:9-17). He therein learned about the grafting in of the Gentiles into the family of God. He was shown that he must literally "Go into all the world and preach the Gospel to every creature," (Mark 16:15).

A new revelation is when God brings us to a new understanding of Himself or of His Word--an understanding which we didn't have before and were having trouble arriving at. When God reveals something to us which we didn't know before, it's new to us, but not to Him. Any revelation from God which we might receive is already given in the Bible. When we find it out, it becomes a "new revelation" to us.

Peter's trance was given for the purpose of enlightening him to a more full sense of the Great Commission, a sense of it which his natural thinking would not receive easily by itself. Jesus brought him "up hither" to a more perfect understanding via this trance.

Peter's understanding, up until then, was that it was unlawful for him to eat anything common or unclean--that is, for him to fellowship with non-Jews. The Old Testament laws prohibited Jews from associating with other nations except under some very strict guidelines. But Peter judged the spirit of the vision, and as providence unfolded, he saw God in it.

All dreams, visions, and revelations of God, have a biblical base somewhere, though often they seem not to at first. If we would allow some time for the interpretation to come forth (through a great variety of possible ways, as shown in Chapter 5), the Spirit Who authored the message will manifest.

I dreamed that I saw an internationally-known minister walking, upset and complaining. He was saying, "I'm tired of those ministers on television always talking about God!" Upon waking up, I said, "Lord, this message doesn't seem to be scriptural, nor have I ever heard this minister say anything like that. I know he is a truly anointed man of God, a televangelist himself, who appreciates other men of God being on television. But what does this dream mean?" I didn't discard it just because it jarred my thinking.

As I pondered this dream, I sensed God was in it. Somehow I knew there was a message from God for me in it. Within a few moments I remembered that I had recently thought a similar thought, in my real life, deep down in my heart. Then I immediately understood that God had heard my thought and was repeating it back to me through this minister whom I respect. He too, I was sure, felt the same way.

When I had thought, "I'm tired of those ministers on television always talking about God," I was intending they should give the people God, and not just talk about Him. I think Christian television programs should have a bit more Holy Ghost action in ministry to people than they do, and not just words. However, my thought, and my dream, was only referring to those who "only talk" and they're not all like that.

I believe the dream came forth not only to show me that God had heard my innermost thought, but also to show me that He agreed with me. It is scriptural to teach and preach, and thereby persuade all men everywhere to repent, (Acts 19:8; 28:23). It is also scriptural to give the people God through power demonstrations inspired of His

Spirit, and not just talk about Him. I also believe that the startling form of the dream was able to come in the way it did because God knew I would find His Spirit in it, if not in the message.

When the Apostle Paul had a night vision of a man directing him to Macedonia, he might have questioned whether it was inspired by God, (Acts 16:9). He had a mind to visit the churches in Asia Minor which he had established earlier and see how they were doing. In the natural, he might have thought that the devil was trying to thwart his endeavours. The fact that he saw a vision of a man, and not of an angel of the Lord, didn't help him to test the spirit of the dream to determine if it was of God.

Yet in verse 10, he immediately moved to obey that revelation, being satisfied *in his spirit* that the Lord was directing him to Macedonia. Paul proved the spirit of the vision, and the Holy Spirit clearly bore witness with his spirit that this was God's will.

There are many dreams of God chronicled in the Bible with which we can compare our dreams to determine if ours are scriptural. But if our dreams do not seem to exactly follow the biblical records, they may yet be of God. The spirit behind our experience must coincide with and give the same testimony as those in the written Word of God. These are given and handed down to us for examples, for our personal admonition, instruction, and learning. In addition, the spirit of prophecy is the testimony of Jesus, (Revelation 19:10). So too, the spirit behind prophetic dreams must testify of and magnify the Lord Jesus Christ.

In these last days, many "new revelations" falsely so-called are being spoken just like in Bible times. Thank God we can confound and put to shame all liars and enemies of the Cross of Christ through the living Word of God and with true visions and revelations therefrom--just like in Bible days!

In these last days we will have a greater outpouring of the Spirit of God than ever before, therefore greater experiences of a supernatural nature. The biblical examples serve as the base from which God will launch that which He will manifest in fullness through us in the last days.

We are to reject any dream, revelation, supernatural experience, or any teaching which contradicts or in any way tends to bring us away from the written Word of God, the Holy Bible. Satan and his ministers are transforming themselves into angels of light as never before, (2Corinthians 11:13-14). False prophets and ministers are multiplying in the world (Matthew 24:4-5) introducing doctrines of devils (1Timothy 4:1-2) and they must be rebuked and confounded, (Galatians 1:6-9).

God is giving the Body of Christ in this last generation spiritual discernment as never before. We are to know them who labour among us in spirit and in truth. God will always confirm His uncompromised unadulterated Holy Word with signs and wonders following (Mark 16:20) to demonstrate His Spirit with power (1Corinthians 2:4) and to exalt Jesus Christ so that all men will be drawn unto Him, (John 12:32).

Judging Dreams

1John 4:1 (author's paraphrase) Beloved, believe not every dream, but try the dreams whether they are of God: because many false dreams are gone out into the world.

Beloved, receive not every dream, but test the dreams. Often dreams from God are quickly identified and easily discerned. When we're not sure if a dream is of God, the following pointers can help us to try the spirits.

1) The Inner Witness

Romans 8:16 The Spirit itself beareth witness with our spirit, that we are the children of God.

The Holy Spirit of God teaches us all things and guides

us into all truth. When we are first born-again He teaches us that we are the children of God. As we mature, He teaches us other things--anything we need to know--including which dreams are of Him. This "inner witness," God's testimony in us, is the primary way by which we can discern whether a dream (or anything else) is from God.

2) Peace

Colossians 3:15   And let the peace of God rule in your hearts, to the which also ye are called in one body; and be ye thankful.

Dreams from God will, as a rule, bring peace to us and not leave us upset, disturbed, or confused. Even when they contain chastisement, there's an underlying sense of peace because the Lord is still with us. An exception to this, understandably, may be when one is willingly disobeying His will.

3) Joy

Luke 1:44   For, lo, as soon as the voice of thy salutation sounded in mine ears, the babe leaped in my womb for joy.

Mary, with Jesus yet in her womb, visited her cousin Elisabeth, with John the Baptist yet in her womb. When Mary greeted her, John leaped for joy at Jesus' presence, and the Holy Spirit manifested Himself, (Luke 1:39-44). As John rejoiced in Elisabeth's womb when Jesus was near, so we too may rejoice when His voice, His message is present in a dream.

4) Praise

Daniel 2:19   Then was the secret revealed unto Daniel in a night vision. Then Daniel blessed the God of Heaven.

Dreams from God bless our souls and inspire us to praise Him. We'll awaken with Him on our minds and with a thanks offering on our lips. An exception to this may be when He gives us a weighty, sobering message, perhaps one of judgment or imminent danger.

5) Comfort

Psalms 94:19   In the multitude of my thoughts within me Thy comforts delight my soul.

Of all the thoughts in my dreams, those which are of God comfort and delight me. Those which discourage and disturb me are not of Him.

6) Quick and Powerful

Hebrews 4:12   For the Word of God is quick, and powerful, and sharper than any two-edged sword, piercing even to the dividing asunder of soul and spirit, and of the joints and marrow, and is a discerner of the thoughts and intents of the heart.

The Word of God is quick, and has "above-natural" power. When a thought comes quickly, faster than you could have consciously conceived it, and it comes with a force above normal for your own mind, it is probably inspired by God. A message from God in a dream may be similarly "quick" and "powerful" so that you must admit that your own mind could not have conceived it naturally. Of course, it must also be scriptural.

7) Light

1John 1:5b   God is light, and in Him is no darkness at all.

There is a glory to visions and dreams of God--a special glory, a brilliant light, a glow, a shine, a radiance, golden rays, brightness, splendour. Dreams and visions of God

may have a degree of these (often a great degree), especially supernatural ones.

8) Edification

1Corinthians 14:3 But he that prophesieth speaketh unto men to
edification, exhortation, and comfort.

A dream from the Lord, like a prophecy, should leave
you with an overall sense of being edified. Though it may
contain an exhortation of some kind, it should end with a
measure of comfort--if indeed it is sent by the Comforter,
(John 15:26).

9) Sensing Good or Evil

Proverbs 4:18-19 But the path of the just is as the shining light, that
shineth more and more unto the perfect day. The way of the wicked is
as darkness: they know not at what they stumble.

If at first you cannot discern a dream, see which path it
travels on as you ponder it--toward the light (God), or
toward darkness and stumbling (the flesh or the devil).
Ultimately behind all things there is either a sense of *the
eternal* if God is in it, or a sense of *the pit* if He's not.
Appearances to the contrary notwithstanding, there are no
shades of gray between the white and black--all things,
ultimately, are either good or evil.

While sleeping face down once I physically felt as though
somebody threw a sort of wet rag on my back. As a reflex
action, my right leg lifted up at that moment, bending at
the knee, and I awoke. Still laying in bed, I started talking
with Jesus in my heart, asking Him to help me discern
whether that was of Him or of an evil spirit.

It then occurred to me that Jesus wouldn't do me that
way--He doesn't surprise His people with devices which
cause fear and doubt. It then occurred to me that there
was more of a sense of the pit (darkness) than of the

eternal. Then I knew just what to do. I bound the devil in the Name of Jesus, and went back to sleep.

Incidentally, on that occasion I was in someone else's home. This can and does occur on one's own property, but it's less likely to. We have more authority on our own property.

10) Life or Destruction

John 10:10 The thief cometh not, but for to steal, and to kill, and to destroy: I am come that they might have life, and that they might have it more abundantly.

Abundant life from the Lord, or a destructive device from the devil: ultimately behind a dream is one of these opposing extremes, as with light and darkness.

11) Spiritual Presences

When a supernatural experience involves a spirit coming upon you in a literal and tangible way, as could happen in a trance, you may understand it to be of God if it approaches you from above, or of the devil if it approaches you from below.

A Christian woman who was sick in bed was attacked by an evil spirit trying to kill her. She noticed how his visit commenced at her feet first, and how the *lifelessness proceeded upward.* She did die, and went to be with Jesus, but she was raised from death by other Christians who were with her praying in the Name of Jesus. And that spirit left her retreating *downward.*

While visiting Tulsa, Oklahoma, some time ago, I experienced a trance during a time of prayer in a Church. As I lay prostrate, it seemed a spirit, an angel of the Lord, fell upon my head first and quickly filled my entire body with his *presence coming downward* right to my feet. A supernatural vision was given me in which God confirmed several things. It ended with the angel leaving my body feet first, and quickly going *upward* and finally releasing my head.

As the angel of the Lord departed from me, the word "CONFIRMATION" in capital letters was left with me. (I had been asking the Lord for a confirmation on some important matter, and that was His response.)

By the direction from which a spirit approaches you, you might discern where he's coming from, and who sent him. Yet even in these areas there are exceptions because Satan, the prince of the power of *the air* (Ephesians 2:2), often launches fiery darts therefrom. And the Holy Ghost with fire has been known to anoint people *from the feet upward.* Therefore, each case warrants spiritual discernment to some degree.

12) The Anointing

2Timothy 3:5   Having a form of godliness, but denying the power thereof: from such turn away.

A dream may seem to have an organized or pleasant form or sense to it. But if it lacks the anointing (it denies the power of the Holy Ghost) He's not in it.

13) Simplicity or Subtilty

2Corinthians 11:3   But I fear, lest by any means, as the serpent beguiled Eve through his subtilty, so your minds should be corrupted from the simplicity that is in Christ.

If a dream involves subtilty, and lacks the simplicity that is in Christ, He's not in it.

14) Congruency or Confusion

Ecclesiastes 5:7   For in the multitude of dreams and many words there are also divers vanities: but fear thou God.

Ecclesiastes 5:7 (niv)   Much dreaming and many words are meaning-less. Therefore stand in awe of God.

If a dream contains many unrelated words, pictures, ideas, and spirits, it's not inspired by God because God is not the author of confusion, (1Corinthians 14:33). On the other hand, when dream-thoughts come together like clockwork, or the parts are consistent one with another, or they flow with an end to make a point, the dream is probably from God.

15)   Discrepant Dreams

Matthew 12:25   And Jesus knew their thoughts, and said unto them, Every kingdom divided against itself is brought to desolation; and every city or house divided against itself shall not stand.

A dream divided against itself shall fall, and not stand. Though a dream which has discrepancies within it may seem to stand while it's taking place, it will eventually begin to fall--either when we awaken, or in the next few hours or days when it doesn't prosper.

God's Word shall prosper in the dream whereto He sent it and accomplish something pleasing, though it may be gradual. It may be for an appointed time, but at the end it shall speak and not lie. We may trust in it, and wait for it, because it will surely come to pass, (Habakkuk 2:3). His message will not fall or return to Him void, (Isaiah 55:11).

16)   Shepherdless Dreams

Zechariah 10:2   For the idols have spoken vanity, and the diviners have seen a lie, and have told false dreams; they comfort in vain: therefore they went their way as a flock, they were troubled, because there was no shepherd.

False dreams don't comfort--though at first they may seem to comfort us in the flesh (the carnal mind). Jesus said, "By their fruits you shall know them," (Matthew 7:20). And the fruits of false dreams are vain comfort, trouble, and a scattered, shepherdless flock.

17) Recurrent Dreams

Genesis 41:32 And for that the dream was doubled unto Pharaoh twice; it is because the thing is established by God, and God will shortly bring it to pass.

God often repeats His dreams and visions in order to establish His messages in us. He tripled to Peter the vision of unclean animals in a sheet descending from heaven, (Acts 10:9-16). The Lord doubled to Joseph the dream of his brothers bowing in respect to him, (Genesis 37:5-11). The second time that Joseph had this dream, it was with different symbols, and with a greater revelation--namely, that his father and mother also, along with his brothers, will bow in reverence to him.

When we receive a message more than once, though the symbols may be changed, it may be God establishing His will in our lives. If we're not sure, we should diligently inquire of Him because something is trying to establish itself in us when it begins repeating itself. When a message from God in a dream or vision is given to us two or three times in a short space of time, such as in one night or within one week, it may be an indication that God will shortly bring it to pass.

18) Discerning Ears

Job 34:3 For the ear trieth words, as the mouth tasteth meat.

We may speak our dream into the air and see how it comes into our ears. If it's of God, the words will quicken our spirits, (Psalms 119:50). We may even speak it to another Christian, if the Lord permits us, and see how it bears witness with them, how it "tastes" to them.

I have often had dreams which I didn't think meant too much. As I would speak the dream to myself and to the Lord, or to the person it concerns, I would learn that it had a real significance.

I dreamed of a certain minister thinking I had received a very general word of knowledge for her. Talking over the phone with her, I said, "I really don't think this dream means too much, but..." And as I shared it, God's presence began to manifest, the interpretation came forth, and prophecy flowed. A very weighty message concerning the Middle East was given her. As I began to speak, the Holy Spirit used my words, and they tasted increasingly good to us.

My nephew Victor dreamed that the Lord Jesus Christ was talking to his younger brother, Chris, and that there were some lambs nearby. He didn't think the dream was God-inspired because it didn't come in a spectacular form, he didn't go into a trance or anything like that, and because he didn't think Jesus would honour him with a revelation from Heaven in a dream.

But the dream "tasted good" to my ears as he shared it with me. Not only because it appeared like a dream which Jesus would inspire, but it bore witness to my spirit, and it also confirmed some other dreams about Chris which I had received from the Lord. Also, as Victor shared the dream, he showed an excitement and a fluency in his voice and a brightness in his face. This too helped me to discern that the dream was of God.

19) Discerning Eyes

"The eye trieth sights, as the mouth tasteth meat." If the ear can test words as the mouth tastes food (Job 34:3), then certainly the eye can similarly test sights (images, visions, dreams) to see if they're of God.

As the mind is being renewed to the Word of God, so is the spiritual eyesight. The spiritual eyesight then becomes conformed to and at home with godly sights, and seeks to abstain from all "appearances" of evil. When a spiritually-minded person sees an ungodly view (such as a dream not inspired by God), his spirit responds, "I've not so learned Christ," (Ephesians 4:20). That is, "This dream does not agree with what I have learned about Jesus Christ. This view doesn't taste good to my eyes. This image doesn't fit my picture of Christ."

When a dream or vision is inspired by God, it "tastes good" to the spiritual eye in the same way that the Word of God tastes good to the spiritual ear.

20)   Fragrance

Psalms 45:8   All Thy garments smell of myrrh, and aloes, and cassia, out of the ivory palaces, whereby they have made Thee glad.

The "spiritual fragrance" which a dream seems to bring with it may indicate who sent it. If the fragrance hints of the Rose of Sharon, or the Lily of the Valley, or sweet perfume, or some other pleasant aroma which speaks of Christ, it is of Him. If a dream sends a bad smell, it is from the devil.

The fragrance of a simple dream may be nothing more than imaginary--it only seems to "smell" good as you think on it. However, the fragrance of a supernatural dream can be more than imaginary. You might literally smell the actual presence of the one who inspired it with your physical nose--either while you're still dreaming, or when you wake up.

21)   Glory to Jesus

John 12:32   And I, if I be lifted up from the earth, will draw all men unto Me.

Ultimately behind any message, Jesus Christ, the preaching of the Gospel, and the Holy Bible, must be magnified and praised. A dream (or any other experience) which plainly or subtly declines or shies away from these is not from God. Also, any revelation which equates Christianity with other religions is not from God, (Galatians 1:6-9; Ephesians 1:19-23; Philippians 2:9-11; Colossians 2:6-9).

22)   Prophecy fulfilled

Jeremiah 28:9   The prophet which prophesieth of peace, when the word of the prophet shall come to pass, then shall the prophet be known, that the Lord hath truly sent him.

One basic rule for determining whether a prophetic dream (or a prophecy) is of God is to see it fulfilled. However, there are exceptions to this rule because although it will eventually come to pass if it is of God, it may be a long time before it does. Prophetic messages are largely conditional, they depend on other factors in order to come to pass. So before a prophecy, vision, or dream comes to pass and demonstrates that it is of God, we should test it by some of the other principles shared here. Then we can know if it's of God before it comes to pass.

In addition, the devil can come as an angel of light and show us portions of the future too, at times. If we believe his messages are from God only because they come to pass, we will be deceived. We should always try the spirits by several of these principles, and not just by one or two. And God's messages will stand up to all of these measures which He has instituted in His Word.

When we can discern whether a revelation is of God before it comes to pass, we may be in a position to get in concert with it and help it come to pass. Our degree of discernment, knowledge, and yieldedness, can hasten a move of God.

23)   No Spiritual Presence

The absence of evil may be an indication that the Lord is

present. If you don't perceive that God is in a dream, but you don't perceive the devil in it either, God may yet be in it. If the devil is in it, it won't be long before he raises his ugly head seeking to influence it, or seeking attention. But when God is in it, He doesn't always demand attention. The Holy Spirit has been called the Shy Person of the Godhead because He knows how to order things aright without all the time making Himself known. So when there is nothing unscriptural or disturbing about a dream, we may at least begin to trust that God is in it, at least until further notice is given.

Now there are natural dreams in which neither God nor the devil are involved. In these we should sense a humanness, a naturalness which lacks the presence of any spirit, and we may conclude that they are products of our own natural minds.

24)   Anointed Ministers

A dream may be from God when it features anointed spiritual leaders such as apostles, prophets, evangelists, pastors, or teachers. You may see them on television, you may read their books, or you may know them personally. You highly esteem them in the Lord, therefore you are more inclined to receiving God's messages through them-- in your dreams and visions as well as in your real life.

25)   Familiar Presence

The spirit behind a dream should not be completely foreign to us. If it is, it's not of God. The Holy Spirit may speak through diversities of impressions, feelings, images, words, or any combination of these and possibly other means. But He is still God, and we should be able to recognize our Good Shepherd's voice, howsoever He may be pleased to speak.

26) Confirmation

A dream may be from God when the message and the symbolism used is in your league. A confirming dream will agree with other leadings of God and with circumstances in your real life. It will fit right in and line up well with your present understanding of God's Word and of His will for you.

Not every dream from God is a *confirming* dream. He may disclose *informing* dreams too. Dreams, visions, and prophecies which contain new information can be challenging, and they must be checked out. Those revelations which confirm a matter which you already know about are much easier to discern and say "Amen" to.

Chapter 7

Some Experiences

Psalms 17:3 Thou hast visited me in the night.

The following are some additional experiences which I have had in sleep. Again, attention is due the Author of the dreams, and not the dreamer. The Bible says that God is not a respecter of persons, He has no favourites, (Acts 10:34). What I have experienced, many other people have experienced, and anyone can experience. As you read, learn some of the ways of the Spirit and hear what He is saying to the Church. At the same time, let your heart become excited and expectant to receive like experiences.

1) Choices

I dreamed I was in the hallway of a large building where many people were walking in and out of different rooms, through the corridors, and up and down the stairwells. They were all seeking their proper places in the building. They were to hurry up and decide which room they would enter, and once they did they would not easily be able to change their minds.

The Holy Spirit greatly impressed my inner man with the word "CHOICES." He was indicating that any major decision or choice we make in these last days (concerning ministry, business, our natural lives, etc.) would be final and unchangeable--with the possible exception of a very few special circumstances.

There was a great cloud hovering over the building, and its thick threatening darkness showed that there was a great imminent storm. Two young women which I know in real life were helping an elderly woman who could not help herself to get into her proper place of refuge. They were not forced to rush as some of the other people because they had made prior preparations for such a state of emergency, and the Holy Spirit said of them, "Prepared." In reality, these two women of God have such a ministry, and I am satisfied, as the Spirit said, that they are prepared for what's on the horizon and are also helping others to be prepared.

Some of the people had made unwise choices, and could

not make a change. Others were trying to change their settings and it cost them. Still others had made wrong moves and were suffering irreparable loss.

There is a great storm on the horizon in the realm of the spirit, and it will have many repercussions in the natural realm. We will experience hints of what is to come in fullness during the Great Tribulation Period. We know that there are many great blessings which God is getting ready to manifest before then, on behalf of His own people. But the storm in this particular dream represented turmoils which are about to hit the earth.

Upheavals, revolutions, catastrophies, confusion, and chaos is coming in governments, economies, societies, religions, and in every area of life. Our only escape is in Jesus, and our only course to victory through the storm is in walking by the leading of the Holy Spirit, in the perfect will of God, in the place He chooses for us. Anything that can be shaken, will be shaken. The fire of God shall try every man's work of what sort it is, (Hebrews 12:25-29; 1Corinthians 3:10-15).

When I awoke, I knew this was a message for the global Body of Christ. I shared it with several prophets and they each told me it was for the whole Body. Brethren, God has always sounded an alarm in His camp to alert His soldiers of what was to come. Today He is repeating the alarm, "Prepare ye the way of the Lord; steer right paths for Him, and not wrong ones," (Matthew 3:3 author's paraphrase). Thousands of people will fall in these endtimes and thousands of plans will fail. But destruction shall not come near the saints of God who abide in Him.

Psalms 91:8-12 Only with thine eyes shalt thou behold and see the reward of the wicked. Because thou hast made the Lord, which is my Refuge, even the Most High, thy Habitation; There shall no evil befall thee, neither shall any plague come nigh thy dwelling. For He shall give His angels charge over thee, to keep thee in all thy ways. They shall bear thee up in their hands, lest thou dash thy foot against a stone.

2) Saved from Wrath

I dreamed I was in a great big building (the world) which was on fire and falling apart. Many people were trying to escape, but could not. I was in a boat (Christ, the Ark of our salvation) being driven by a stream of water (the Holy Spirit), and a young lady (the Church) was sitting in the boat with me. The course of the stream was not predictable, but it was the only safe place within that building.

I saw some young men and preached the Gospel to them, trying to compel them to enter the Boat. I pointed to the fires below (hell) to warn them how close they were to being burned, but they wouldn't take heed. Finally, the Boat ascended (was "caught up") into the air and approached a window (the heavens were opened) to meet the Lord in the air. The window was the only exit by which we could escape the troubled building. A great light (the glory of the Lord) began to shine through the window. Then I awoke.

A Great Tribulation Period is reserved for this earth, during which time the wrath of God will be poured out upon sinners. But those in Christ (the Boat, the Ark of our salvation) who are in the flow of the Holy Spirit, will be saved before that Period, (1Thessalonians 4:16-18). However, until then, we will see, and even now we are seeing, glimpses of the judgments yet to come, for they have already begun. We must compel others to come into the Ark so that they too can be saved.

Luke 14:23   And the Lord said unto the servant, Go out into the highways and hedges, and compel them to come in, that My House may be filled.

3) Blessings

I have also seen, in dreams and visions, many blessings from God coming down from Heaven in behalf of His obedient people. I would see great miraculous healings and deliverances, and massive salvation crusades in public places. I would also see lost arms and legs restored, cripples healed, the demonized set free, and lost sinners saved by the thousands.

Many times the Lord has shown me tidal waves, floods, and heavy rains of His Spirit pouring down throughout the earth. The Prophet Hosea says that the Lord will come unto us as the rain.

Hosea 6:3   Then shall we know, if we follow on to know the Lord: His going forth is prepared as the morning; and He shall come unto us as the rain, as the latter and former rain unto the earth.

4)   The Gift of Faith

Once I saw the *gift of faith* in operation--every prayer request was immediately and explosively granted. God was showing me that He is moving powerfully now to answer His people's prayers and meet their needs. I have also seen the *whole armour of God* upon the Body of Christ, and lightning from heaven coming down upon and consuming our enemies as we march on proclaiming the Gospel.

5)   Spiritual Cassette Recorder

It's one thing to receive messages from God, and it's another thing to share them. As we learned earlier, with regard to Joseph's dreams, we shouldn't be too quick to share the secrets God reveals. But I have often sensed a liberty to share some of the revelations God has given me. I would freely share those of blessing, but I have hesitated to share the judgments coming because I didn't want to disturb or depress anyone. In prayer, I had been asking the Lord whether or not I should share these too.

Then I dreamed that I saw an audio cassette recorder with a blank tape in it. The recording mode was on, and the tape rolling, able to record any words spoken into the microphone. I was directly in front of the machine facing it and ready to speak.

Clearly, the Lord was telling me to proclaim what He has revealed--the blessings, and the judgments. He used a cassette tape recorder because He knew I would understand it correctly. I record messages all the time, and the machine in the dream looked exactly like the one I actually use.

6) The Wills of Peoples

I had seen an evangelist on television testifying of a mighty outpouring of the Spirit of God which he witnessed among the Japanese. On the program, he shared from Acts 16:6, where the Holy Ghost had placed a sort of ban on the Asiatic countries and directed the Apostle Paul and the Gospel westward to Europe. From there, the Gospel of the Lord Jesus Christ was brought across the Atlantic Ocean and spread throughout the Americas. This is why the Western Hemisphere is largely evangelized, and the Far East as a whole is not.

During the meetings in Japan, God spoke to the evangelist saying, "The ban on Asia is lifted." In other words, from now on we can expect to see the Gospel prosper in the Far East as never before. Millions of Asians will turn to Jesus virtually overnight. Hallelujah!

I was so excited by this message that I looked at my map of the world, especially at the continent of Asia. Then I started asking God, "How, Lord? How are You going to do this? How is it possible? There's so much to be done. So little time. So many giants against us. How will we ever win these nations to Jesus?"

A few weeks later, I had the following dream: I saw that same evangelist sitting behind a desk and saying to me, "The way to win the nations to Jesus is, you've got to change the will of the people." I asked God for understanding in this, "How does a person change the will of a people?" He answered my question with a question, "Why did I use that particular evangelist to make that statement in your dream? What does he represent?"

Then I understood. He is a Christian changing the wills of peoples around the world so that they may come to accept Jesus. He does this not only by preaching, teaching, and praying for them, but also by donating schools, churches, medical facilities, and funds to those who need them. He not only talks about God, he also gives the people God in a tangible way, in a demonstration of the heart of God.

Sometimes actions speak louder than words. As with the evangelist, and as with God Himself, all Christians must so love the world that we will give them what they need from God, for we've got the God they need. This is the way to preach the Gospel to the poor--the spiritually poor, and the materially poor. This will change the wills of peoples and win them to Jesus. They'll be willing to come to Jesus. "My people shall be willing in the day of My power," (Psalms 110:3a author's paraphrase).

7) Tongue of Fire

As I walked through my neighbourhood on my way home one afternoon, the streets were filled with many sinners. I was disturbed at seeing them because I had preached unto them many times before, and felt it would be fruitless to again try to warn them to turn from their wicked ways. I felt powerless, and the cause seemed hopeless. So I went home.

I laid down to take a nap, and a supernatural anointing came upon me. My spirit stood up, while my body was still lying down, and a large single flame of fire descended from Heaven and appeared directly over me. With my head inclined upward, my tongue was caught up to that fiery flame, and up to Heaven from which it came.

All of a sudden, my spirit man was encircled by some members of a church I'd been attending. They saw me and said, "Something's happening to David. What's happening to him? Let's ask the pastor. She'll discern this for us."

While they were talking, I was thinking to myself, "Good, they're calling the pastor. She'll discern. I don't want them to cause me to come back into the natural realm just now. I hope they yield to what the Spirit is trying to do." I realized, even then, that I had the ability to either stay in or come out of that experience.

The pastor looked at me, squinting her "eagle's eyes," and said, "It's God. Let's see what He wants to do." I thought to myself, "Oh, good." Then everyone of them fell on their backs in yieldedness to what God was doing.

My spirit went further out into the air and then stood at one of the street corners in my neighbourhood, through which I had just walked. All the sinners in the area were able to see me in the middle of the street, and I boldly preached to them. My head was still inclined toward Heaven, and my tongue still caught up to the flame of fire coming down from Heaven. I don't know what I was preaching, but the anointing of the Holy Ghost was spilling all over the place and convicting everyone of their sins and of their need to accept Jesus.

Hundreds of people came running from everywhere. As they came within five to six feet of me, the Holy Ghost fell on them and they fell out on their backs. As they dropped, unclean spirits cried out with loud voices coming out of many people which were vexed with them. And in the same exhalation, the people commenced to speak with other tongues and magnify God as they laid all over the streets. And of the rest of the people--those who stood afar off to watch in amazement--no one dared to come near because a great fear fell on them all. And the Name of the Lord Jesus was magnified--in Brooklyn, New York!

Without supernatural acts of the Holy Ghost in demonstration as the Early Church experienced, there's no way to reap the endtime harvest of souls for Jesus. The Word of God which we preach is ALIVE and full of POWER. The Gospel of Jesus Christ is the POWER of God unto deliverance. God confirms His Word with POWERFUL SIGNS AND MIGHTY WONDERS.

The mantles of POWER which rested upon the apostles and prophets in the Bible are coming upon and clothing God's End-Time Army. We have tried to work the works of God in our own power--and failed! God's Word tells us we can't do it in our own might or power, but only by the demonstration of His POWERFUL Holy Spirit. The great Apostle Paul testifies:

1Corinthians 2:4-5   And my speech and my preaching was not with enticing words of man's wisdom, but in demonstration of the Spirit and of power: That your faith should not stand in the wisdom of men, but in the power of God.

Zechariah 4:6   Then he answered and spake unto me, saying, This is the word of the Lord unto Zerubbabel, saying, Not by might, nor by power, but by My Spirit, saith the Lord of hosts.

As at the beginning of the Church Age, this latter move of God at the end of the age will not lack the supernatural. Read the entire Book of Acts--I like to call it "The Book of Actions"--and study these verses: Acts 2:1-4, 14-21; 3:19; 4:31; 5:11-16; 6:8; 7:55-56; 8:5-8.

8)   Anointed Ministry Materials

I received by mail a catalog of ministry materials from a particular evangelist. I read it through and went to sleep, then the fire anointing of the Holy Spirit manifested all up and down my body as I would awaken, then sleep, awaken, and sleep. I saw that preacher high in the air with great glory shining around and through him.

In the spirit, I saw many of his books, tapes, record albums, Bibles, prayer cloths, and his ministry items which I had just examined in the catalog, and the glory of the Lord shone in them as well. It seemed that anyone who would come into any sort of contact with this minister, his ministry, or his materials, would be touched by the anointing of God in some special way--in salvation, healing, deliverance, or blessing of some kind.

As I was beholding marvelous revelations about his ministry, my physical body was actually experiencing shaking, quaking, and rolling about on the floor under this supernatural anointing. This lasted over four hours. I also saw two other preachers with him, and they were all looking at me and talking about me. They spoke of my past, my present situation, and my future.

The reason why I share this experience is to show the reality and power of the mantles of anointings on God's true servants. We often take them for granted. Our familiarity with preachers--their books and tapes, their prayers and points of contact--can easily breed a contempt for them. In the time of Moses, the children of Israel began to despise the manna which came from Heaven, and the pleasant land which God gave them, (Psalms 78:22-32; 106:21-25).

Some of God's people today are likewise despising their inheritance in Him, and are therefore having difficulty in receiving blessings from Him. But if we would remain spiritually-minded, always acknowledging the Spirit contained in the items He anoints, we can more easily embrace them, and more easily receive from God through them.

Many Christian homes are blessed with an abundance of Christian materials: teaching tapes, worship tapes, powerful books, anointed oils and other points of contact, and of course several versions of the Bible. Yet Christians still have many needs unmet. Our faith can reach the level that instead of seeking for a minister to lay hands on us and pray or prophesy to us in order for our blessing to come, we will be able to touch his prayer cloths, read one of his books, or listen to one of his tapes, and receive our blessing.

We don't always esteem anointed points of contact as highly as we ought, so we miss some things. And certainly not every religious article is anointed. But when we see their true spiritual worth and appreciate the anointings which are there, they can easily supply our needs.

Acts 19:11-12   And God wrought special miracles by the hands of Paul: So that from his body were brought unto the sick handkerchiefs or aprons, and the diseases departed from them, and the evil spirits went out of them.

Isaiah 10:27   The yoke shall be destroyed because of the anointing.

Matthew 9:29   According to your faith be it unto you.

9) The Labourers and the Homeless

In an out-of-body experience during the Spring of 1986, my spirit entered a church building where a woman of God was ministering to some Christians at the altar. She was operating in the gifts of the Spirit. I got on the prayer line, and I recognized a minister whom I really know. The people she was ministering to had knowledge in the things of God--they were not newly converted babes in Christ-- yet they all wanted God to touch them through this woman's ministry.

As I saw some of them go down under the power of God as they were blessed, I was praying, "Lord, let me go down too; touch me one more time, Lord, bless me too." Then I looked up and saw Jesus above the church building watching over us, but also observing things outside of the church. The inside was full of glory, the outside was dark and gloomy.

Then Jesus looked outside of the church where there were sinners but no Christians, and He asked me, "Where are all the labourers?" Then He said, "There sure are a lot of homeless." He seemed to be very concerned about them.

I came back into my body (without being prayed for by the woman of God in the vision) and began to meditate on this revelation. I realized that many labourers are not out labouring--they are in church enjoying God's blessings. There is a time for church, and a time for blessings. But after we have received a portion from the Lord, we should go out and spend it on the harvest of souls outside the church.

As to Jesus' statement about the homeless, it did contain revelation to me. Even though I had already known that there are a lot of homeless people, I didn't know how great the problem of homelessness in America really was. But it certainly was the word of the Lord for the hour because the following week, as a confirmation, a news team broadcast a week-long series on the plight of the homeless in America.

News reports and documentaries covering the plight of the homeless have dramatically increased since then. And I believe Christians have been called out to labour for the harvest more urgently since then.

10) Angelic Song of the Great Commission

In a trance, a choir of angels appeared to me and sang the Great Commission mandate to me, (Mark 16:15). One of them came forth toward me and sang these three specific verses, each in a different tone of voice:

"Go ye into all the world and preach the Gospel to every creature." (He sang this first verse in a regular orderly way.)

"Many profess that they do it, but they are not really doing it." (He sang this second verse with greater force and seriousness.)

"Pour out the Spirit!" (His third verse was most bold and wild, almost violent, and intense.)

I understand that the first verse relates to the Early Church Period, when Jesus first commanded His disciples to "Go and preach." The second verse speaks of the history of the Church, throughout which there were many false Christian leaders leading astray the flocks of God, professing to preach the Gospel but not really doing it. The third verse applies to the present time, during which the Spirit of God is ready and looking for vessels through whom He can manifest and pour Himself out in fullness.

In my own life, I can relate these verses to a series of moves of the Lord which I have experienced. Soon after I was saved, I was pressed in the spirit to "Go and preach the Gospel to everybody." Over the years, I have seen many people who "profess to be preachers of God, but are not." Most recently, a bold, almost lawless Spirit has come upon me emboldening me to move in the Spirit and "let Him pour out and have His way!"

The Church of the Lord Jesus Christ commenced with the command to preach the Gospel. Throughout history we have seen many wolves in sheep's clothing, and many true Christians not doing their jobs. But this is the time that the Holy Spirit will pour out unbound. And it is the time for Christians to move out into the fullness of the Spirit, and let Him have His way.

11)   The Blood of Jesus Christ

In a supernatural dream, I saw Jesus in the sky in great splendour and glory. Every eye on earth was beholding Him. Then I heard an angel's voice ring, "The Blood of Jesus Christ shall appear unto all very shortly." Then I awoke.

One of the signs of the last days is blood in the sky. In Joel 2:30, this blood is Jesus' Blood. The outpouring of the Spirit of God involves the manifesting of the Blood of Jesus to convert sinners. It is His Blood which washes our sins away, (Revelation 1:5).

12)   The Redemption of Their Soul is Precious

While asleep one night, I was praying with groanings and spiritual travail for my nephew Victor. I awoke, still praying, and heard Jesus say, "The redemption of their soul is precious." I sensed the Lord was referring to all of my family, but that He was showing me this particular relative as an example.

Shortly thereafter, supernatural anointings began to visit

Victor and his whole life was transformed. In less than three months he became a missionary. And as he preached the Word of God and ministered to people, the Lord would confirm His Word with signs and wonders following. Souls would be saved, believers filled with the Holy Spirit, the sick healed, devils cast out, and other miracles would manifest.

Sometimes we don't know just how far-reaching even a simple revelation of the Lord can be. But if we would follow it all the way through, and not despise that which may at first seem small, we will behold great and mighty things which we, as yet, know not of. Jesus said that the kingdom of God is like a tiny grain of mustard seed which was sown and became a great tree; and the birds of the air came to live in it, (Luke 13:18-19). "The redemption of their soul (and their seed) is precious," (Psalms 49:8 author's paraphrase).

13) Jewelry Wearers

Natural dreams can be mistaken for spiritual ones. A lady dreamed that everyone wearing jewelry missed the Rapture of the Church. Her pastor preaches very strongly against women wearing jewelry, lipstick, make-up, and slacks. I believe that her strong personal beliefs prompted that dream. There are many true Christians who use these things and they are not going to miss the Rapture.

If her dream was inspired by God, those who missed the Rapture were symbolized by jewelry-wearers because God knew she would interpret them as sinners, and sinners will miss the Rapture. The fact that she applies the jewelry-wearing (which symbolizes sinning here) to everyone who wears jewelry, including Christians, does not mean that God used the wrong symbol.

God can use the viewpoint of our own human prejudices in order to speak to us in a dream or vision at our own level of understanding. However, when He does this, we are not to assume that He is necessarily agreeing with or endorsing our prejudices.

As I shared in Chapter 5, God speaks to us on our level of faith and understanding, but He wants us to always be growing in both. He wants us to compare spiritual revelations with scriptural truths in order to interpret His messages accurately.

14)   Immodest Gospel Singer

I dreamed that a female Gospel singer was wearing tight black leather pants while singing for the Lord on television. I believe God was revealing that some Christians use their liberty for an occasion to indulge the flesh--they often take their Christian freedoms to an extreme. They appear as and appeal to those who are still in the world under the dominion of sin. Therefore, they fail to convict sinners and bring them to repentance.

Yes, we have liberties. But we should stay far enough on the modest side of things to avoid making provision for the flesh or causing another to "stumble" in their spiritual growth.

Romans 13:14   But put ye on the Lord Jesus Christ, and make not provision for the flesh, to fulfil the lusts thereof.

Romans 14:21   It is good neither to eat flesh, nor to drink wine, nor any thing whereby thy brother stumbleth, or is offended, or is made weak.

Isaiah 52:11c   Be ye clean, that bear the vessels of the Lord.

15)   A Succubus

I was dreaming of an attractive young lady. I began to desire her, and to caress her. As I did so, I perceived a swarm of bats encircling and closing in on me. I willed myself to resist the temptation, and the bats receded. This was an actual experience of spiritual warfare in the spiritual realm, as we discussed in Chapter 4, under "Spiritual Warfare."

As I thought of how much control over the situation my own free will had, I again yielded to the lust of the flesh to see if the bat-like demons would return. They did, so I resisted them again and began to cause myself to awaken.

Then I thought I'd test them one more time to see if they really were behind this dream. I yielded again and they again began to close in on me, this time more forcefully. I determined to resist them more forcefully and to awaken fully, which I was able to do.

Now awake, I still sensed evil in the air, so I called upon "The Blood of Jesus, in the Name of Jesus," and acknowledged the ministry of angels working in my behalf. The evil then dissipated fully. I learned that we must possess our souls and command the mind of Christ to reign over us in the night seasons.

I have heard several testimonies of persons, even Christians, being attacked in the night by wicked spirits trying to have sex with them. These are the *succubi* which we identified and defined in Chapter 3, under "Sexual Dreams." Sometimes their attacks are so forceful that they can be felt physically, and even seen. Often such demons are huge, though there are many different kinds and sizes of them. However, they would always have to leave when "The Name of Jesus" was enforced against them. Every knee must bow and every tongue must confess that He is Lord, (Philippians 2:9-11).

Today there is a staggering amount of people who are helpless to resist supernatural visitations of the devil in sleep because they don't know the power of Jesus Christ. Brethren, we must learn to use our God-given power and authority in Jesus Christ.

Jesus said:

Luke 10:19 Behold, I give unto you power to tread on serpents and scorpions, and over all the power of the enemy: and nothing shall by any means hurt you.

Paul prayed:

Philippians 3:10   That I may know Him, and the power of His resurrection.

16)   The Name of Jesus

Several years ago, when I was first learning about the power in the Name of Jesus, I was asleep one night. At first I didn't understand what was really happening, but a demonic spirit began to torment me and cause nightmares. I would cause myself to awaken, collect my thoughts, and go back to sleep. Another nightmare would come, and I would do the same thing.

This happened about four or five times until, finally, I became so angry that I got up and stood in the middle of my room authoritatively commanding the devil to leave "In the Name of Jesus!" Well, he left, and about ten minutes later I went back to sleep without being disturbed again that night. Praise God!

When we're at rest, we are open to spiritual things and the devil tries to enter our lives then. But he cannot stand against the power of Jesus' Name. And every Christian has the right to use Jesus' Name to enjoy victory in every area of his life.

Mark 16:17   And these signs shall follow them that believe; In My Name shall they cast out devils.

17)   Demonic Blindness

While beginning to fall asleep one night, I felt a spirit coming upon my head and covering my eyes. I knew it was a spirit but it wasn't a familiar presence to me--it was the first time I'd perceived that particular kind of presence. I asked God for discernment, and I didn't get paranoid and rush to rebuke the spirit. I knew that God often comes to us in new ways to teach us to be flexible and skillful in the discerning of spirits.

I decided I sensed more evil than good, but chose not to cast him out yet, until I was absolutely sure. I fell asleep and dreamed that I was blind, and I was very uncomfortable. Now sure it was a demon affecting my head and eyes, I woke up and cast him out in the Name of Jesus.

If I had decided before I fell asleep that he seemed to be more evil than good, I should have cast him out then. Sometimes we've got to act upon what we believe at the time, even if we're not absolutely sure we're right.

18)   Demonic Sinus Congestion

One morning as I awoke from sleep, I felt a demon jump off of my face as soon as I opened my eyes. He had been congesting my sinuses as I slept, without my knowledge. I only realized what had happened after it happened, as when a person realizes that an air conditioner has been on only when he hears it turn off. And instead of commanding the spirit to leave my face, I only commanded him to stay out of my face.

19)   Praying for Osvaldo in Sleep

While in New Jersey for a meeting, I had to sleep on a convertible sofa, sharing it with a Christian brother from Cuba. Osvaldo is one of the boat people who survived the exile from Cuba in 1981. He has also survived, by the grace of God, many fights--in prison and on the streets. In one fight, he received a cut on his face which left him with a long scar from his forehead, down the side of his face, to the side of his neck. God's hand has been on this young man because He has a special purpose for his life. Amen.

As I slept near him, I dreamed I was gently touching someone and praying that God would bless him. I woke up and realized I was sitting upright on the bed with my hand on Osvaldo's face. This was more than just a *visual* dream.

This was an *actual* experience with my spirit during sleep because my spirit, by the inspiration of the Holy Spirit, instructed and led my body's movements.

I was startled and laid down again to go back to sleep, hoping he hadn't felt anything. Later that day, Osvaldo told me that he knew what had happened and that it blessed him. He felt it was inspired by God. I think that God was intending to show His closeness, His gentleness, and His concern for him.

20) Pentecost Coming

The next night, again sleeping near Osvaldo, I was dreaming about the final outpouring of the Spirit of God which will occur before Jesus returns. The words "PENTECOST COMING" (in capital letters) came to me clearly in that dream. While dreaming, my physical body literally quaked under the power of the Holy Ghost, causing me to awaken for a moment, after which I would go back to sleep. This happened about three times.

After the third time, I remained slightly awake and noticed Osvaldo similarly quaking under the power of the Holy Ghost. It occurred with him about three times also. Later that morning, he told me he knew that I had quaked, but he didn't know that he had quaked as well. I told him God was revealing that His Spirit is coming upon "flesh" in these last days, and that men will literally quake under His power as the saints of old.

Acts 4:31   And when they had prayed, the place was shaken where they were assembled together; and they were all filled with the Holy Ghost, and they spake the Word of God with boldness.

21) Judgments

In dreams and visions, I have seen many judgments coming on America. Once I saw many large, live nuclear missiles directly over the United States, indicating vulnerability, openness to nuclear attack. In 1987, I saw America beginning to engage in small battles with other countries, and eventually engaging in larger battles. I saw a financial crisis wherein few people had jobs, and those without jobs couldn't find one except through a miracle of God. I've seen earthquakes occurring in New York and California.

I'm not a prophet of doom, but in a supernatural dream, I read several reasons for the great hurricane of 1992 which devastated a large portion of Miami, Florida. The first reason for it, typewritten in capital letters, was the word "JUDGMENT," indicating it was a demonstration of the judgment of God.

22) The Sacred Blood

In a dream, I saw a church where all the people were engaged in natural conversations, unedifying talk. I spoke to the Lord asking Him to remove me from there, then I found myself flying through the ceiling and meeting the Lord in the air.

This was no longer only a dream--my spirit was now actually out of my body. I saw Jesus, and He spoke to me in a language which my natural mind could not understand, but which my spirit understood perfectly as though He spoke in English. He was giving me instructions about something, and I was nodding to indicate that I understood Him. I flew further out into the air and saw my neighbourhood below, and then I asked Jesus, "Where are we going?"

. He then caused me to dive swiftly downward and into an apartment where I saw two large demons behind some ornamental hangings on the living room wall. (Of course, not all ornamental items have demons attached to them.) Somehow I knew that the Lord had sent me there to cast them out.

I first addressed the more powerful one because I knew that once he was defeated the other one would be quickly defeated also. All I said was, "The Blood of Jesus! The

Blood of Jesus! The Blood of Jesus!"--repeatedly. At first they laughed at me, then they cursed me with spells, then they threw some slimy substance like mud at my face, which I was able to feel. The spirit of man has tangibility and can feel spiritual substances.

At this point, I thought unto the Lord, "What should I do, Jesus? I can actually feel this stuff?" I sensed He wanted me to persist, so I kept on repeating "The Blood of Jesus!" against the larger demon, with my eyes staring penetratingly into his. I knew that if anything can overcome demonic forces, it's "The Blood of Jesus" because He is the true Prince of the power of the air.

Finally, the demon loosed his hold on that home. He came down off the wall and fell completely flat on his face before me, and as he was falling, he screamed "Aaahh, the SACRED BLOOD!" Then I turned to the other demon and claimed "The Blood of Jesus!" against him, and shortly he fell in defeat too.

With my spirit still out of my body and in this strange apartment, I asked the Lord, "What now? Should I fly into one of the other rooms to see if there are any humans to preach to or pray for? Should I make a confession of faith that those who live there will be saved? Should I pray a special blessing upon that home? What now, Lord?" My spirit felt like a conqueror, and rightly so.

Then, with an overwhelming force, the Spirit of God drove me out of that apartment, back up into the sky, and back down into my body, as though I had no say in the matter. Now fully back in my natural body, my natural mind said, "Wow! That was powerful!" Then I praised the Lord for His power over all the power of the enemy. Ever since then, when I engage in spiritual warfare, I often claim "The Sacred Blood of Jesus" against the devil and his cohorts, as he had taught me. And "The Sacred Blood of Jesus" always wins.

Revelation 12:11   And they overcame him by the Blood of the Lamb.

23) Invisible Imposter

In another out-of-body experience, I found myself in the air, but I didn't see or hear anything. I spoke to the Lord, "I'm out here, Jesus, but I'm looking for You, waiting on Your leading. I'm not going to endeavour anything on my own."

As I waited to see what would happen, still meditating on the Name of Jesus, I saw two arms approach me from below, seeking to hold hands with me. The arms were wearing open sleeves, white, as though the person was wearing a robe, like Jesus--but I couldn't see his face.

I thought, "Ah, this seems like Jesus, except that He doesn't hide His face from me--He has nothing to hide. Maybe He's trying to teach me how to discern Him in a new way." So I clasped his hands and flew with this mysterious supernatural being--but still, no face.

Then I thought, "Hmm. Something's not right. Let me claim "The Blood of Jesus" and see what happens. If this is Jesus, there'll be no problem--if not, I'll expose and rebuke this imposter." (Notice how my spirit was able to think, speak, and move, even though I was out of my body.)

As I did so, I could see an ugly facing appearing on this being. He became frightened and in torments, and started pleading with me to let him go. I wrapped my legs around his body, tightened my grip on his hands, looked directly into his eyes, and said, "No! You wanted to hold hands, so let's hold hands a little while longer, until I say so!" I commenced to torment him with "The Blood of Jesus," then released him and came back into my body.

24) Supernatural Intercession

While praying on my knees one night, a special anointing came on me and my spirit left my body. I entered the guard's office of a prison and saw guards mocking and harassing an innocent inmate, trying to provoke him to fight back so that they could really hurt him. He covered his face and head with his arms as they punched him and struck him with clubs. (Of course, not all prison guards are like these.)

While being bullied, the victim begged for mercy, and as they continued striking him, I could feel the blows he was receiving upon my own spiritual head and body. Then I was tempted to fear, and thought, "Jesus, I can really feel these blows. Am I in danger? Might I get hurt? Should I draw back from this experience and get back into my body?" My own will may be involved to a certain degree, and can choose either to yield to or resist such kinds of experiences.

Then Jesus said to me, "It's alright, you can't get hurt, I'm with you. This is SUPERNATURAL INTERCESSION." Now encouraged, I thought, "Well, Praise God! If Jesus is with me, let me give myself to it even more so," and I "willed" myself to enter into it more fully. ("Glory!") I was literally *standing in the gap* in the realm of the spirit, on that man's behalf.

In intercession we are often "touched" with the feeling of another person's infirmities, (Hebrews 4:15). Our spirit, by the strength of the Holy Spirit, takes hold together with that person against their problem. As a result, we can almost literally feel what they are suffering. This involves comforting the feebleminded, supporting the weak, bearing others' burdens, and weeping with them that weep--all through intercession in the realm of the spirit. And it also involves rejoicing with them that rejoice!

If we don't understand this, we'll decline from this degree of prayer and limit God from moving by His Spirit. But God wants us to give ourselves unto these things of the Holy Spirit, with knowledge, and with faith.

25) Flying Anointing

Early one morning at about three or four o'clock, I had an angelic visitation and an out-of-body experience. In it, my spirit literally flew in an angelic rocket ship which was being piloted by an angel. As we travelled around the second heavens (outer space) he was teaching me some things about planets and space and time. Some of his statements were witty and humorous, and I felt like a youngster in grade school.

As I slowly returned and came back into my body, a tremendous presence of brilliance and power was all over me and in my room. When that en-trancing and flying anointing was lifted, I could only remember three simple statements which the angel had made. Though he had spoken much more to me--he was teaching throughout our whole trip--I only retained a little thereof. And within a little while, I no longer felt the supernatural presence.

Later that day, at about three or four o'clock in the afternoon, I was ministering in the gifts of the Spirit in a local church in New York City. I laid hands on a lady and prayed for her to receive the Holy Ghost with the evidence of speaking with other tongues, as she had asked me. When I laid hands on her, she instantly spoke with other tongues one specific word--something like "Shalamahia! Shalamahia! Shalamahia!"--about five or six times.

It was so distinct that when this lady stopped I asked if she could interpret it because it seemed it might be a message from the Lord. She declared she didn't even know that she had spoken with other tongues and that all she knew was that as soon as I laid hands on her she went flying out of her body!

I believe that the "flying anointing" which had visited me on that morning and gave me an out-of-body experience was still resting upon me without me knowing it--and she unwittingly tapped into it. When we prayed asking God to bless her, He answered and gave her an added blessing as well--more than she asked for!

A supernatural visitation from God can contain many kinds of anointings and cause many kinds of blessings to manifest. The person so visited will certainly receive an impartation of the Holy Spirit. And those unto whom he ministers can also be partakers of those same anointings.

26) Deadly Anointing

In a tremendous trance, I saw a vision of my friend Terri with an awesome presence of God's anointing upon her. As she stood near her pastor and other people from her church, it seemed as if she was his bodyguard (for she does indeed intercede in prayer for him). The presence of God was resting so powerfully upon her that it seemed as if anyone who would approach her or the pastor with an intent to do harm would instantly drop dead before her.

I could best describe it as a dreadful, dangerous, almost deadly anointing, and I was afraid to approach her in this vision. When I knew that she discerned I was friendly, I then approached and talked with her with more calm and confidence.

When I awoke from this trance, I could feel the fiery presence of the Holy Spirit all over me and in my room for several hours afterward. So I immediately called and shared this revelation with Terri and encouraged her to walk boldly in the knowledge that God has given her great spiritual authority in the Body of Christ. Because she is a humble person, I had to explain the vision several times before she understood the impact of what God was disclosing.

Only a few days later, God promoted Terri in her ministry of prayer. She began leading a team of women intercessors, and was publicly acknowledged and author-ized by her church elders. The Lord brought into natural manifestation what He had just recently revealed. Surely the Lord God will do nothing without revealing His secrets unto His servants the prophets, (Amos 3:7). And the fact that the vision came with a tangible anointing of fire shows us there was to be an actual impartation of the Holy Spirit upon Terri for her new ministry.

From this supernatural revelation, I understand that God is anointing His chosen people in a powerful way in these last and evil days. He wants to enable us to quench all the fiery darts of the wicked so that nothing shall be able to hurt us. God is saying, "Touch not My anointed ones, and do My prophets no harm. Or else My Anointed One will touch you and do you harm!" (Psalms 105:15).

This revelation also gives me a glimpse of how God sees Terri in the spirit. We are to know them which labour among us and are over us in the Lord--after the spirit, and not after the flesh, (2Corinthians 5:16; 1Thessalonians 5:12). There is great order and blessing in the House of God when we know our neighbour's true calling and rank in the army of the Lord, and salute and honour them.

27) Three Secrets

I preached in a church in Westmoreland, Jamaica. That night, after falling asleep, the Spirit lifted me up out of my body and I was caught up in the realm of the spirit. I came before the pastor of that church, and her spirit shared three secrets with my spirit--two were complaints of weakness, and one was a petition to visit the Holy Land which she had presented before the Lord.

The next morning, before flying back to New York, I visited her to find out if the revelations were true. We are not supposed to believe in every spiritual experience we may have, but to test each of them carefully.

I already knew this experience was of God because there was much great light, peace, and power, and everything else in it also seemed to be of Him. But I wanted to make sure, and I also wanted to encourage her and let her know that God hears and will answer her prayers.

She immediately affirmed the validity of the weaknesses, but denied she had the petition I said I heard. But I was sure this was of God, so I kept pressing her to try to remember. Finally she admitted, "Oh, yes. I did pray that to the Lord once. When a missionary visited Jamaica many years ago and testified of a marvelous trip to Jerusalem which she had just enjoyed, I secretly prayed in my heart, 'Lord, I'd like to go there some day.'"

I rejoiced to see a complete confirmation of the revelations. When she affirmed that the secrets were true, we prayed that God would bless her in these areas, and thanked Him.

28)   Time Tunnel

While asleep, an angel appeared to me extending his hands and telling me to go with him. My spirit arose trusting him by faith, took hold of his hands, and went flying with him. As we ascended airward, I could pick up some sounds in my neighbourhood, and heard two policemen talking by way of walkie-talkies. One of them was reporting from his patrol car and said, "It's quiet out here, everything's peaceful. I think I'll take my lunch break now."

As with the prophets of old (2Kings 6:8-12), God's people today can, at times, see in the realm of the spirit and know by supernatural revelation what certain people are talking about in private. As the Spirit of God allows us to, we can see and hear in the realm of the spirit and know supernaturally things which are really happening, and things which shall be.

Then we travelled through a time tunnel into the future and landed at an airport. This commercial airport, which was somewhere in the United States, was guarded by military police, and didn't have a lot of people there. Few people were allowed to travel. I think some of our airports are headed toward this type of setting.

29)   Secret Church Meetings

I dreamed I was going to a meeting in a large office building. I arrived at the meeting room, entered, and sat down. Then I saw someone at the front of the room addressing the group. The meeting had all the appearances of a secular conference. There were no crosses, Bibles, or other religious articles, and the people there did not seem to be Christians.

All of a sudden, it dawned on me that everyone at the meeting was a Christian, including the speaker, and that this was a Church meeting taking place under the guise of a non-religious one.

From this I understand that there are now, and may continue to be more, secret meetings of the Church--even in America. There are some things which the Lord wants to say and do which will not be open to the general public, and which will not be advertised. There are some persecutions coming against the Church and its leaders, and some devices of the devil too. But the Lord would have us to employ certain strategies to outmaneuver them all and stay ahead of the enemy.

30) Angelic Turntable

While asleep, I heard a record playing on a turntable in the realm of the spirit. First I heard the "click" sound of the "automatic play" dial, then the lifting of the needle arm, the dropping of the record album onto the turning plate, and the resting of the needle on the turning record. Heavenly music began to play in stereophonic sound. I heard angels singing in the background, and one of them moved forward and sang a specific message to me. One of the things he said was, "And your wife is on the way...but you'll have to make the final decision for yourselves." (I'd been praying for a wife.)

31) Chinese Print Shop

In an out-of-body experience, the Spirit of the Lord brought me to mainland China. While out there, I was able to think and to reason within myself almost normally. I realized that God was not intending to give me any specific revelation concerning China, but simply wanted me to see that land from the air.

I saw people as they went about their normal daily business around their cities and villages. As the Lord began impressing me that He wanted to bring me back into my body, I asked Him if He would please give me a moment more in that realm. I wanted to see a detail which would teach me something that I didn't know before. I sensed the Spirit saying, "Okay, but just a small moment more."

I then flew over a street with some businesses on it and entered a print shop. In it were several old-fashioned printing machines in use. Then, because those machines were a prominent detail, I immediately understood that many of those business shops have little or no modern equipment. Then the Spirit led and brought me back into my body.

As I meditated on that experience, I understood that a great percentage of many businesses and homes in China are using outdated machinery and technology from decades ago. They are generally poor and are seldom able to obtain the latest high-tech equipment available. Afterward, I inquired and found out that this is indeed the situation in China.

From this experience, and others like it, I also understood that it is possible, at times, to communicate with the Lord in the realm of the spirit, to ask Him questions, and to make requests. At times, the Spirit of the Lord will completely order each aspect of a supernatural experience, and not permit our input. At such a time, we must be very "swift to hear and slow to speak," (James 1:19). It is extremely easy to grieve the Holy Spirit by speaking or moving out of turn during such an experience. I'm learning this by experience.

However, there are times when we may enter the realm of the spirit and enjoy heavenly conversation with God. It is neither difficult nor unlawful to ask to fly here, to go there, to see this, or to hear that, in that realm. The kind of supernatural experience which the Lord initiates, and what it involves, can be flexible and unpredetermined. It may hinge upon our knowledge of spiritual things, our right heart motives, our devotion to Jesus, our faith, and our own free wills.

Before the Patriarch Moses saw the angel of the Lord in a flame of fire in a bush which burned but was not consumed, he had said, "I will now turn aside, and see this great sight," (Exodus 3:3). Before the Prophet Habakkuk heard the audible voice of the Lord, he had said, "I will watch to see what He will say unto me," (Habakkuk 2:1). After the Apostle Paul had experienced supernatural disclosings of the Lord, and gained an understanding about them, he was able to say with confidence, "I will come to visions and revelations of the Lord," (2Corinthians 12:2).

32)   African Song

I dreamed I was in Africa and danced in the spirit as I heard anointed music playing in the tropical rain forests. Then an African man approached and sang to me in an African dialect. I could not understand the language, so I tried remembering some of his keys words to bring them back with me into the natural realm.

Then it seemed as though I had grieved the Holy Spirit by trying to remember the words, so He stopped the message bluntly and woke me up. He had wanted me to simply receive the message into my spirit. However, I did remember two specific words and an African minister later helped me to understand one of them. Being interpreted, it partly related to my earthly pilgrimage at that time.

33)   A Minister Praying

I dreamed a minister was praying in the hallway of an auditorium. Inside, there were many Christians likewise praying and seeking God. As the minister sat and prayed near the open doorway, others were entering the auditorium to begin praying and seeking God too.

I understand that it is through the prayers of the Body

of Christ, and our leaders, that we draw people into the House of the Lord.

34)   Anointed Lightning Bolt

While asleep with my hands on my stomach, I saw and felt a lightning bolt shoot out of my left palm and into my lower abdomen. I believe this means that through my weakness (left hand) the power of Christ (lightning) will manifest in my inward spiritual man (abdomen). This was an impartation of the anointing of the Holy Ghost within me, intending to strengthen my inward man and enable me to go on in the things of God. (Lord, send Your power!)

35)   Firecracker in the Spirit

I was alone in church one night sleeping in the lobby next to the entrance. I could vaguely hear people outside as they walked by. Early in the morning hours, when there was no noise, I was sound asleep. Suddenly a loud blast sounded right next to the door near me and startled me, throwing my mind into a dither. It was around the Fourth of July, so it had to be some kind of firecracker. I'm sure the devil used somebody to do that to me without their knowledge, and I was greatly disturbed.

I went into the sanctuary and lay on the carpet before the altar asking God to fix my mind so I could sleep in peace. That big firecracker really blew my mind. I went back to sleep and in a few minutes I heard another one, louder, and right next to me at the altar. I awoke and realized it was a spiritual sound, not another literal one. I also realized that my mind was back in shape and my thoughts were more comforted. I'm convinced an angel "fought fire with fire," so to speak, and countered the devil's work with a similar device in the spiritual realm. Praise God!

36)   Sleeping on a Heavenly Cloud

During a week of special church services, I had been unjustly offended publicly. At the end of the week, God ministered to me by a message given through an anointed preacher. The entire message to the congregation was as a needed meal from Heaven directed personally to me. I became encouraged and felt refreshed. I had been fed!

That night, I slept on someone's living room floor, but it seemed as though I'd slept in Heaven. From the moment I fell asleep to the moment I awoke, all I sensed around me was a heavenly cloud, and God's love. Praise the Lord, for He gives His beloved people heavenly sleep, (Psalms 127:2).

If someone wrongs you during the day, don't fret. At least you know you can sleep well, your conscience is clear, Jesus is with you. You can lay down and sleep in peace knowing that the Lord will sustain you in the night with heavenly peace and blessed sleep. And in the morning you can look up and direct your prayers up to Him with confidence.

Psalms 5:3   My voice shalt Thou hear in the morning, O Lord; in the morning will I direct my prayer unto Thee, and will look up.

37)   Talk to Me, Jesus!

While in consecration before the Lord once, I was boldly requiring of Him clarity, confirmation, and direction. In so many words I prayed, "Jesus! Jesus! Jesus, talk to Your servant. I need You. I need to see You. I need to hear You. Help me. God, I'm going to sleep now, and the devil can't visit me. You, my Lord, will speak to me what You know I need to know."

I firmly laid both hands on my head and boldly said, "Talk to me Jesus! Talk to me Jesus! I agree with and obey whatever You say, Lord, just talk to me now Jesus! Amen.

I went to sleep and had a dream which clearly confirmed

God's specific leading in my life at that time and showed me where I was spiritually. Several unquestionable details were also involved.

I always ask the Lord to speak to me in dreams (and in other ways) but rarely have I done so with such great boldness. I have done so only out of desperation. He has answered each time. I think we should be sensitive to the liberty that the Spirit gives us, and be bold in this way only when we are compelled by need. What we say and do in our prayer business in God's presence, we shouldn't do presumptuously or simply because we heard someone else's testimony.

Ask the Lord to speak to you in dreams, and in other ways too. He will. But don't pray with a serious and compelling fervency unless your situation demands a serious and compelling revelation.

Chapter 8

Supernatural Dreams and Trances

Acts 11:5a In a trance I saw a vision.

Definition of Supernatural Dreams

In the preceding Chapters, we have seen that the sleeping state can be a more spiritual dimension than the waking state. This is why God often chooses this time to communicate with men. As Christians, we can learn to use the Word of God to bless us during sleep and enlighten us to God's perfect will for us. We can receive simple wisdoms, insights, and blessings from God in dreams all the time because the Holy Spirit is always with us.

As we fellowship with our precious Lord in the night seasons, He answers our questions, explains and clarifies situations, meets our needs, and reveals many things to us. These things may be in our spirits by the Holy Spirit, and may even border on the supernatural. Yet they are not necessarily supernatural dreams.

A supernatural dream should be defined as one which Jesus directly inspires--and He doesn't do this every night. Nightly blessings in fellowship with the Holy Spirit in dreams certainly involve Jesus, but in a more indirect way. Keep in mind, though, that there are many gray areas here, so a clear distinction cannot always be made. When a definite revelation is experienced, such as hearing or seeing Jesus or an angel, seeing things to come, receiving a new anointing, and similar manifestations of a spectacular nature, then it is a supernatural dream.

In supernatural dreams, there is a weightier and more peculiar presence of God. There are different spirits, kinds of anointings which come upon us in supernatural dreams. There are also special angels sent forth to minister for us in such dreams. Therefore, it is more difficult to be interrupted or otherwise influenced by natural or external factors when experiencing a supernatural dream.

There are angels of divine revelations, or "messenger" angels, of whom Gabriel is chief. These are they which visit us in the night on the special occasions of supernatural dreams. And, of course, these angels minister for us in day visions too. On regular nights, we still enjoy the ministry of the angels which are always with us.

On many occasions, I have perceived the angels' ministry for me before, during, and after sleeping. Some time ago, during a lengthy consecration time before the Lord, my spiritual senses were awakened to acknowledge the angels. As I slept, their presence around me was so intense that I didn't move all night long, for fear of grieving them. Of course, I could've moved without disturbing them, but I didn't want to miss out on anything of what God was doing. His precious presence around me all night was as great pillows cushioning my body completely.

Cushioning speaks of comforting (as the Comforter, the Holy Ghost, is sent for, John 14:26), hiding (as in the secret place of the Most High, Psalms 91:1), and also protecting, (as from the fiery darts of the wicked, Ephesians 6:16). God always protects His people. But when we're opening up and yielding ourselves unto the Lord in consecration, particularly when fasting, the devil may try to visit us and deceive, disturb, or destroy. Therefore, God provides protection for us supernaturally.

Many times while getting ready to lay down and go to sleep, I would see flashes of light upon my bed: at the middle, at the foot area, and especially on the pillow. I believe these are just glimpses of the angels sent forth to minister for me in the night seasons, (Hebrews 1:13-14). They are with me throughout my sleep, and often help me to wake up.

Once I felt a flaming finger touch my thigh, causing me to awaken. I have heard hands clap in the spirit, an alarm clock ringing in the spirit, an angel whistling, angels singing or playing music, Jesus Christ clearing His throat ("Ahem-ahem"), and Jesus calling my name, ("David").

There are distinct differences between the voices of angels, the voice of the Holy Spirit, and the voice of Jesus. These are just some of the ways God often chooses to awaken or otherwise minister unto His people.

God sustains us in sleep by His ministering spirits which have special charge over us to keep us, (Psalms 3:5; 34:7;

91:11). The angels give us encouragement, insights, and instructions. They have touched me, shown themselves to me, and sung unto me. They have sung some messages to me, and they have also allowed me to hear them praise God.

The angels engage in different levels of praise and worship. Not just different kinds, but different levels-- higher, and lower. On the lower levels, they may sing revelations, warnings, and leadings. On the higher levels, they may incline toward Heaven and sing of divine things, address eternal things, and magnify God.

Their companies may be as small bands, choirs, soloists, instrumentalists, symphony orchestras, or any other form of groups. They play unlimited kinds of musical instruments, and can play unlimited kinds of notes, sounds, and combinations. Sometimes their music sounds like that of this world (such as jazz, opera, disco, rock, classical, etc.), and sometimes angelic music is clearly from out of this world. Also, they can combine greatly differing kinds of music and song and symphonize them in perfect harmony.

The fact that angelic music often sounds like the worldly forms (rock, jazz, or any others) is not an endorsement of the latter. Rather, it shows that all music originates in God, regardless of how it may be misrepresented in the earth by Satan and sinners. Remember, Satan has no ability to create new things. Whatever gifts and talents he possesses were given him from above, were "prepared" in him (Hebrew: *kuwn,* "applied, appointed, fastened") in the day he was created, (Ezekiel 28:13).

Personally, I don't prefer the aforementioned forms of music. I enjoy traditional hymns, old spirituals, easy listening, and choir music. But when it's anointed, and especially angelic, I do enjoy it, regardless of what form it may come in.

The angelic ministers bless us every night whether it's supernaturally or not. The best way to enjoy more of their ministries and acknowledge them is to know about their operations according to the Bible, and yield to them with faith and expectancy. Whether or not our experiences are spectacular, we must always believe that our angels are constantly ministering for us because we are Christians.

In dreams, there can be varying degrees of God's presence. The more His presence manifests, the more supernatural the dream is. There can also be varying degrees of Satan's presence--though it's usually not Satan himself, but one or more of his cohorts.

The more that Satan's presence manifests in a dream, the more supernatural (that is, "over" the natural realm) the dream is. On the lower levels of such dreams, you may be uncomfortable while you're sleeping, or you may simply be entertaining carnal thoughts in dreams. You can cause yourself to awaken, then read the Bible, pray in the spirit, and worship God, to remedy this. Then go on back to sleep. Or you can captivate ungodly thoughts and meditate on the Word of God while you're still asleep, without necessarily having to wake up.

On the higher levels of Satan's presence in dreams, you may perceive (by seeing, hearing, and/or feeling) an evil presence, an actual evil spirit in your midst. To remedy this, you must call upon "The Blood of Jesus, in the Name of Jesus," and rebuke that spirit. In these cases where a spirit is actually present, you should cause yourself to awaken so that you can vocalize your summons. But while you're still asleep, your spirit can begin warring on the inside of you against the foe, until you fully awaken and resist him.

Always remember that whatever Satan's attacks may be, Christians always have more power--to rebuke him. The more he comes on the scene, the more heavily Jesus arms us to resist him! (1Corinthians 10:13). Where sin and Satan abound, the grace of God does much more abound, (Romans 5:20).

Purposes for Supernatural Dreams

1) Revelations

The *word of wisdom,* the *word of knowledge,* and the *discerning of spirits,* are some of the supernatural manifestations of God's Holy Spirit, (1Corinthians 12:8-10). The word of wisdom is a revelation from God about the future, and the word of knowledge is one concerning the past or the present. In the discerning of spirits, the Holy Spirit discloses spirits, thoughts, or motives. They may be angelic, demonic, or human. They may be another person's, or one's own. They may be good, or evil.

These *revelation gifts* of the Holy Spirit may operate in dreams as well as in the waking state. People may dream of the past, of the present, or of the future. In a dream, one may discern where another person is coming from, and what, if anything, he really has up his sleeves.

Matthew 2:12 And being warned of God in a dream that they should not return to Herod, they departed into their own country another way.

God sent a warning in a dream to these wise men from the East who visited the young Child Jesus with gifts. Contrary to their itinerary, they were instructed to return home another way without seeing the evil King Herod again. Any one of a great many kinds of dreams could have been experienced, but basically the revelation involved the discerning of spirits, and a word of wisdom for direction. They were shown a safe path by which to avoid danger.

Matthew 2:13 And when they were departed, behold, the angel of the Lord appeareth to Joseph in a dream, saying, Arise, and take the young Child and His mother, and flee into Egypt, and be thou there until I bring thee word: for Herod will seek the young Child to destroy Him.

Joseph, Jesus' legal father, is hereby warned about the evil king in much the same way as were the wise men from the East. Here, the angel of the Lord is specifically identified as the messenger. Again, the revelation involved the discerning of spirits, and a word of wisdom for direction. And when it was God's time for this holy family to return to Israel, an angel of the Lord again appeared to Joseph to direct him, again in a dream, (Matthew 2:19-21).

In dreams from God, I have occasionally discerned the spirits of churches, of ministers, and of individuals, even the thoughts and intents of the heart, (including my own). I have also been directed where to go, and where not to go. Once, with a mind to travel to a certain state, I dreamed of not going in the season. The Lord told me that if I would go there at that time I would be "robbed." How, or by whom, I don't know. But He's lookin' out for me-- and for you too. ("Thank You, Jesus.")

Matthew 27:19 When he was set down on the judgment seat, his wife sent unto him, saying, Have thou nothing to do with that Just Man: for I have suffered many things this day in a dream because of Him.

Here, Pontius Pilate's wife had discerned in a dream that Jesus was a just man. Though she knew little about Him in the natural, her troublesome dream sufficed to convince her of His innocency, and compelled her to warn her husband. If she'd had spiritual dreams in the past is not known, and how spiritual a person she was cannot be determined. But there was no doubt in her mind that this dream was a supernatural revelation from God. That's why Pilate tried as hard as he did to rescue Jesus from being crucified, and claimed himself innocent of His Blood when he couldn't.

Genesis 20:30 But God came to Abimelech in a dream by night, and said to him, Behold, thou art but a dead man, for the woman which thou hast taken; for she is a man's wife.

Genesis 31:24   And God came to Laban the Syrian in a dream by
night, and said unto him, Take heed that thou speak not to Jacob
either good or bad.

Abimelech, a Philistine king, and Laban, a dishonest
businessman, and others too, were similarly warned of
God in dreams. Throughout the Bible record we find many
accounts of revelations from God coming to people--not
only wonderful, pleasant messages, and not only to saints.
Sinners as well as Christians can receive insights, warnings, and leadings from God in supernatural dreams.

The world conqueror Alexander the Great, the Christian
Emperor Constantine the Great, and other great leaders in
world history are recorded as having made history as a
result of having received revelations from the Most High
God in visions and dreams. These politicians would often
favour the people of God in acknowledgement that He is
the true and living God.

Alexander was going to destroy all the Jews at Judea for
assisting his enemies (in 333 B.C.), but instead reverenced
them and allowed them to go on serving God. A supernatural dream which he had, and one which a Jewish High
Priest had, were responsible for his change of mind.

Constantine legalized Christianity in Rome (in 313 A.D.),
and ended the persecution against Christians which had
been widespread. Supernatural visions, in response to his
prayers, helped him conquer his enemies.

Nicodemus was a public figure who would not approach
the Lord Jesus during the day, for fear of his peers, (John
3:1-2). But he came to Him by night. There are many
people who do not follow Christ publicly, yet they approach Him by night--perhaps on their beds--to inquire
of Him. Shall we say He won't be found of them? Nay.
Didn't Jesus converse with Nicodemus and clarify insights
about the new birth to him?

Today too, there are many people who are outside the
mainstream of God's fold receiving revelations from God
in supernatural dreams and visions. As there were many

Pharisees who believed in Jesus without publicizing their faith (John 12:42; 19:38), even now there are many in strategic posts around the world obeying heavenly visions secretly.

2) Prophecies

Amos 3:7   Surely the Lord God will do nothing, but He revealeth His secret unto His servants the prophets.

Numbers 12:6   And He said, Hear now My words: If there be a prophet among you, I the Lord will make Myself known unto him in a vision, and will speak unto him in a dream.

The *word of the Lord* often came to the prophets via dreams, though the Bible doesn't always state this. God would speak to His servants through dreams, visions, angelic appearances, or by His audible voice. At times, He would speak less spectacularly, such as by the inner witness or impression of the Spirit, or by the still, small voice of the Lord, or by the simple gift of prophecy. The prophets, after receiving God's message from Heaven, would then speak it (prophesy) and thereby cause it to come to pass in the earth.

In the Bible, we see that special ministry gifts, such as apostles and prophets (and, in the Old Testament, the patriarchs too) are the ones who experienced the more spectacular kinds of visions and dreams. Even today this is the rule, particularly when profound, involved messages with much symbolism are given.

Yet in these last days, we will see an explosive increase of visions and dreams in the Body of Christ at large, (Acts 2:17). The ministers, the church members, the mature, the young, whosoever will yield to the Lord, may receive dreams, visions, and revelations from Him, possibly even those of the spectacular sort, so that we may prophesy His will in the earth.

Sometimes dreams show us the future, but that doesn't

mean we or someone else can't change it. God may show us something so that we'll pray about it. He might show us what *can be* if we'll move a certain way, or what *will be* if we don't pray. Prophetic dreams, those which involve the future, are largely conditional. They depend upon our responses.

You may dream that someone got hurt, or killed--but you pray it won't happen, and it doesn't. You may have dreams about upcoming earthquakes, wars, or other disasters, but they may be intended for you to change through prayer. Your relationships with other people, situations in their lives (or in your own), or the conditions or motives of their hearts (or of your own), may be shown in dreams to reveal what needs to be dealt with-- through prayer, or actions, or both. God shows us things not just so we will know them, but so that we will act upon them and order future events.

Three young Christian men had formed a small Gospel musical group. Another young man wanted to join them and, after some prayer, both he and one from this group dreamed that the group consisted of four young men. So he joined.

Soon afterward, the fourth musician desired and asked the Lord for a new set of drums, and then dreamed of a beautiful red-colored set. It wasn't long before he saw the same set in a store and bought it, being satisfied that God was confirming His favour upon the group.

A few months later, this young man's zeal for the Lord began to decrease. He then dreamed that his musical group consisted of three men, as at the beginning. He took this as a warning from God to get and stay "on fire" for the Lord, or else He would remove him from the group. He obeyed God, and the group prospered with God's blessing. Lastly, he again dreamed of a four-man group.

These dreams revealed *what God wanted* for the future of these young men and *what could happen* in their future. Each of these dreams contained a prophetic element which hinged upon the cooperating prayers and actions of the person concerned. So we see how messages from God are often *conditional* and not completely unchangeable. He gives us a vision, a goal, but we've got to do our part in order for it to be fulfilled. Remember, we are labourers together with God, (1Corinthians 3:9a).

There are, of course, prophetic dreams which are destined to come to pass regardless of whatever else may happen. Whether they are personal, collective, or universal messages, we shouldn't try to change such *unconditional prophecies* by prayer or action. Rather, we may pray in order to receive wisdom on how we should respond to or prepare for what's to come.

Occasionally, when God gives me a prophetic dream, I present it back unto Him asking, "What should I do about this? Pray to change it? Pray in agreement with it? Or simply prepare for what's to come?" In His own time and way He explains. But such dreams usually come with instructions already contained somewhere within the context.

Genesis 15:12 And when the sun was going down, a deep sleep fell upon Abram; and, lo, an horror of great darkness fell upon him.

When God covenanted with Abram, throughout Genesis 15, He greatly encouraged and revealed much to him. While a *deep sleep from the Lord* (trance) fell upon him, a most serious unconditional prophecy concerning his seed (descendants) and their future is given to him. Herein he also experiences an *horror of great darkness* which *fell upon him.*

Daniel 7:1-3 In the first year of Belshazzar king of Babylon Daniel had a dream and visions of his head upon his bed: then he wrote the dream, and told the sum of the matters. Daniel spake and said, I saw in my vision by night, and, behold, the four winds of the heaven strove upon the great sea. And four great beasts came up from the sea, diverse one from another.

In this Chapter, Daniel communicates one of the most grave and graphic prophetic dreams chronicled in the Holy Bible. It involves God the Heavenly Father, the Lord Jesus Christ, the Body of Christ of the last days, an angel of the Lord, Alexander the Great, the Anti-Christ, and a host of other prominent particulars.

Daniel 7:15-16 I Daniel was grieved in my spirit in the midst of my body, and the visions of my head troubled me. I came near unto one of them that stood by, and asked him the truth of all this. So he told me, and made me know the interpretation of the things.

In the middle of his body, his spirit was *pierced,* so the original Hebrew word indicates. He was alarmed, agitated, affrighted and vexed; he trembled and palpitated. In short, he went through changes. Then a nearby angel, at Daniel's request, commenced to interpret the dream for him.

Genesis 28:12-13 And he dreamed, and behold a ladder set up on the earth, and the top of it reached to Heaven: And behold the angels of God ascending and descending on it. And, behold, the Lord stood above it, and said, I am the Lord God of Abraham thy father, and the God of Isaac: the land whereon thou liest, to thee will I give it, and to thy seed.

Genesis 28:16-17 And Jacob awaked out of his sleep, and he said, Surely the Lord is in this place; and I knew it not. And he was afraid, and said, How dreadful is this place! this is none other but the House of God, and this is the Gate of Heaven.

Another one of the most supernatural dreams from the Lord recorded in the Bible is this one, commonly known as "Jacob's Ladder," (Genesis 28:10-17). In it the Patriarch Jacob is greatly encouraged and strengthened to endure what is to come. Herein he also receives one of the greatest prophecies of the Bible.

After he awoke, Jacob was afraid, in dread: "afraid" and "dreadful," in verse 17, are translated from the Hebrew word *yare,* meaning "fear, fright, awe, and reverence." Most prophetic dreams chronicled in the Bible, whether they were experienced by patriarchs, prophets, or kings, left the dreamer troubled, amazed, or in awe, for a season. Daniel's cogitations much troubled him and his countenance was altered (changed) as a result of experiencing the supernatural presence of God in a trance, (Daniel 7:28).

Today too, this is not uncommon. As a result of having experienced the supernatural presence of God in a trance, my cogitations would trouble me, and my countenance would be altered. At times, my whole day would be altered because I could not lay aside the dream God had imparted. Yet if a like dream doesn't trouble or amaze us, still it should inspire reverence and holy respect for the Author.

3) Blessing, Healing, or Deliverance

Job 34:24-25 He shall break in pieces mighty men without number, and set others in their stead. Therefore He knoweth their works, and He overturneth them in the night, so that they are destroyed.

Whether they are human beings oppressing and afflicting us, or demonic spirits, God often overturns them *in the night* and heals and delivers us. He removes the wicked ones and sets holy and angelic ones in their place. His blessing may involve a financial miracle, a physical healing, deliverance from evil, the baptism in the Holy Spirit, or even being born-again.

Supernatural dreams can involve almost any type of manifestation of the Holy Spirit to minister unto God's people, and even to sinners. Even the great King Nebuchadnezzar of Babylon was overturned by God in the night, (Daniel 4). After being restored to sanity and to his former position of authority seven years later, the king blessed the Lord for His mighty healing power. He praised Him and referred to His works toward him as great signs and mighty wonders, (verses 2-3). God works great signs and mighty wonders in the night!

4) Enduement of Power

1Kings 3:5, 12-13 In Gibeon the Lord appeared to Solomon in a dream by night: and God said, Ask what I shall give thee... Behold, I have done according to thy words: lo, I have given thee a wise and an understanding heart; so that there was none like thee before thee, neither after thee shall any arise like unto thee. And I have also given thee that which thou hast not asked, both riches, and honour: so that there shall not be any among the kings like unto thee all thy days.

In the context of 1Kings 3:5-14, we see that God supernaturally appeared to Solomon in a dream and covenanted with him. He conversed with him and asked what he wanted. Solomon asked for wisdom to judge and lead God's people. So God anointed him with the gifts of the Holy Spirit which he needed for that task, and He even gave him more than he asked for.

About twenty years later, again in a supernatural dream, God appears to Solomon and answers his thirteen-year-old prayer, (2Chronicles 7:12-22). He herein confirms His acceptance of, and His presence in, the Temple built for His Name. He also offers conditions whereby His mercy shall remain upon Israel. The following popular exhortation to repentance was given to Solomon in this dream:

2Chronicles 7:14 If My people, which are called by My Name, shall humble themselves, and pray, and seek My face, and turn from their wicked ways; then will I hear from Heaven, and will forgive their sin, and will heal their land.

God often clarifies, confirms, commissions, and anoints His people for service in dreams. This may occur as the Holy Spirit desires, or in answer to our prayers. A fresh "Go ye" from Heaven, a new anointing or mantle, various gifts of the Holy Spirit, or even another legion of angels, can be loosed upon us while we're asleep.

Kinds of Supernatural Dreams

I have analyzed my own personal experiences, others' experiences, and most importantly, the Bible. Basically, I have come to understand that there are two main kinds of supernatural dreams, *visual,* and *actual.*

As we saw in Chapter 4, sometimes dreams are simply thoughts, images, and ideas being entertained in the mind during sleep. But sometimes a person's spirit is quite active in dreams and he is actually perceiving or engaging in something in the spiritual realm. This experience is a real one (though it may or may not be visible), and that's why afterward these dreams may seem so real. Even so, not all dreams that seem real *actually* are.

Likewise in supernatural dreams we sometimes see what God is revealing even though we may not be active in the spirit. At other times we are active because an angel of the Lord, or the Holy Spirit, or Jesus Himself, is *actually* manifesting Himself to us, and doing something to us, for us, or with us.

1) Visual

Insights, revelations, warnings, and prophecies from the Spirit of God may come in supernatural *visual* dreams, or in supernatural *actual* dreams. Visual revelations from the Lord in dreams do not require active participation of the person's spirit, or an actual visitation from the Lord. In visual dreams, the person simply observes and receives the message.

Supernatural visual dreams contain more symbols, mysteries, and obscurities, than do actual dreams. The latter, again, involve a literal visitation from the Lord. Therefore, if He comes with a message, it too will probable be literal, and not figurative or symbolic. As a rule, the more supernatural a manifestation of God is, the more clearly will He speak in it.

2) Actual

Supernatural *actual* dreams are those in which God's tangible presence is evident in some way. To *see* the Lord in a dream is *visual,* but for the Lord to *manifest* Himself to you in a dream is *actual.*

A manifestation of blessing, healing, or deliverance, or an enduement of power, requires an actual visitation from the Lord in some form, if the dream is indeed super-natural. Such manifestations involve an impartation of God's anointing which will manifest in the natural realm. Therefore, an actual visitation of the Lord occurs, and active participation of the person also occurs--he literally yields his spirit to the anointing while his body is yet asleep.

If you dream something angelic, and you sense that same presence when you wake up, it was more than just a dream, the angels were actually there. But if there was no angelic presence when you awaken, then the dream was simply visual, though it may still contain a message from God.

And the same can be said of evil presences. When you have a simple visual dream, upon waking up you will not sense that same evil presence (though you should still rebuke the dream). But if you do sense the same presence when you awaken, then there is an actual spirit which you need to rebuke "In the Name of Jesus."

There may be difficulty in discerning whether a dream was either visual or actual. This is because your emotions are affected by your dreams. You may wake up and feel impressed by a dream about Jesus, and therefore you are tempted to believe it was an actual visitation from Him. Your heart is stirred by His *impression,* but it is not necessarily His *presence.*

An unpleasant dream also can disturb you after you wake up, but it does not necessarily mean that there is an actual evil spirit present. Only your emotions feel disturbed because of the evil dream-thoughts.

It is important to know if we just had a dream, or an actual experience in the spiritual realm. By so discerning, we can properly acknowledge and respond to the messages and the presences which may visit us. Different kinds of weapons are used to bind evil messages and presences, and different kinds of faith are used to yield to and receive good ones.

The following experiences are some which may occur while asleep, as well as while awake. The Bible generally refers to these as dreams (when they occur during sleep) but they are really *actual* supernatural *experiences* in sleep. They may be basically different from each other, but sometimes they are similar and manifest together in one message from the Lord.

Apparition:

Here, a person's spirit literally and visibly sees a being who *appears* to him, such as when the Lord appeared to Solomon in a dream by night and conversed with him, (1Kings 3:5). And such as when the angel of the Lord appeared to Joseph in a dream and prophesied to him, (Matthew 1:20).

The highest kind of apparition involves the complete physical manifestation of *a being* to a person or persons by supernatural means. Here, time and space are completely transcended. Many biblical examples of supernatural apparitions describe those of the highest calibre, and they show us that such an experience may involve an angel (a good one or an evil one), the Lord Jesus Himself, or even a human being--if he is still alive on earth--appearing unto us.

(People who have died can be seen in some of our *visual* dreams and visions, but they cannot appear to us in *actual* forms. A supernatural revelation which features a person who is no longer on earth may indeed be an actual experience, only the part of it involving the dead person is symbolic at best.)

In order to tempt Jesus, the devil literally appeared unto Him. He tangibly *took* and *brought* Jesus to Jerusalem and set Him on a pinnacle of the Temple, (Matthew 4:1-11; Luke 4:1-13).

The archangel Gabriel literally appeared and tangibly *touched* Daniel and set him upright, (Daniel 8:15-18). Daniel *saw* him (for he described the angel as a man, in verse 15); he *heard* him (for Gabriel interpreted the foregoing vision for him, in verse 17); and he *felt* his touch, (in verse 18).

When Jesus appeared to His disciples in the Upper Room shortly after His resurrection from the dead (John 20:19-31), He supernaturally entered through the walls, (verse 19). His disciples *touched* and *handled* Him (verse 27), and they also conversed with Him, (verse 28). Jesus literally ate food in their presence, (Luke 24:41-43).

Philip the Evangelist *appeared* unto a man, the Treasurer of Ethiopia, (Acts 8:26-40). He read the Bible to him, preached, baptized him, and then departed from him. As Philip had appeared "out of thin air" (verses 26-27), so also he afterward disappeared "into thin air," (verse 39). This kind of appearance is also known as *supernatural translation, translocation,* or *transportation.* The *appearer,* a human being already on earth, is simply transported to another place. The person so travelling "goes across" the barriers of time and space--he crosses natural laws by an above-natural unction.

Audible message:

Here, a person hears words and sounds supernaturally though no images or visions are seen. Such as when young Samuel was in a *light sleep* and the Lord *called* him. In 1Samuel 3:3-4, the Hebrew word for "laid down" is *shakab,* and in this context it indicates a light sleep. Had a vision accompanied God's audible voice, Samuel would've immediately known that it was the Lord calling him; he would not have thought, as he did, that Eli the Priest was calling him.

Now verse 15 of that Chapter says that Samuel was afraid to reveal the "vision" (what God had "told" him) to Eli. The word "vision" here (Hebrew: *mar'eh*) is defined as "natural sight" or "spiritual sight," and can be literal or figurative. Evidently, in the context of Samuel's revelation, the word "vision" means "message, revelation, or spiritual sight," and does not necessitate a *visual* aspect. The fact that Eli afterward asked Samuel, "What is the thing that the Lord has *said* unto you?" and not, "What has the Lord *shown* you?" further confirms this point, (1Samuel 3:17).

Out-of-body experience:

This is commonly known as "astral projection" and "soul travel." However, Christians should avoid using these terms because they are used by non-Christian mystics and they are not found in the Bible. The scriptural phrases speaking of this experience are: "The Spirit *lifted me up and took me away*" (Ezekiel 3:14); "The hand of the Lord *carried me out*" (Ezekiel 37:1); "The Spirit *took me up*" (Ezekiel 43:5); "He was *caught up* into Paradise" (2Corinthians 12:4); and, "Immediately I was *in the spirit*," (Revelation 4:2).

In this latter case, we must understand that John was *actually* in the spirit because Jesus had summoned him to "Come up hither," (Revelation 4:1). As a result, he was able to behold sights in the Third Heaven, and also on the earth, (verse 2 and onward). Whereas the same term "In the spirit" (in Revelation 1:10) does not speak of an out-of-body experience, as the context in that chapter reveals.

When this occurs, the person's spirit literally leaves his physical body and begins to travel (or, to fly) by the Spirit of the Lord. God must prompt this by a special unction of the Holy Spirit. An out-of-body experience of a high level is usually given with a definite purpose in mind--such as worship, intercession, warfare, prophecy, and other such like supernatural operations. Nevertheless, the Lord may give this kind of experience to a person simply for the purpose of his enjoyment, if He so chooses.

A not so spectacular experience of this is as when the Prophet Elisha told his servant, "My heart *went* with you," (2Kings 5:26). A much more profound one is as when the Prophet Ezekiel was *lifted up* by the Spirit of the Lord and *brought* into the House of the Lord, (Ezekiel 11:1; 8:3). The Apostle Paul also speaks of this kind of experience, (1Corinthians 5:3-4; Colossians 2:5).

There are several conditions under which this can occur, including during sleep. While asleep, I have often been lifted up out of my body by the Spirit of the Lord and travelled in the spiritual realm. Angels would surround and cover my body with a special anointing. At times they would take my spirit by the hands to lift me up out of my body and into the air.

While being literally *in the spirit,* I have arrived at and observed many places, including several nations, such as Mexico, Japan, China, and Africa. Each experience may differ slightly, but several times I have *heard* and *felt* the "wheels" turning while ascending in the spirit, as Ezekiel did (Ezekiel 3:12-14), and also while returning back into my body.

A great variety of *visual, audible,* and *tangible* experiences can be enjoyed in the realm of the spirit, as I will share with more depth in my second book, *Understanding Supernatural Visions According to the Bible.* Please refer to it for a more complete study of audible voices, out-of-body experiences, heavenly visitations, divine sights, and other kinds of visions of the Lord.

3)   Trance

A trance is an actual displacement of the mind wherein one may see into the spiritual (invisible) realm. The word *trance* comes from the Greek word *ekstasis,* which means "ecstasy, a being put out of place, distraction, trance, especially one resulting from great religious fervour; great joy, rapture, a feeling of delight that arrests the whole mind," according to *Webster's Dictionary.*

W.E. Vine, a Bible expositor, defines a trance (supernatural ecstasy) as being "a condition in which ordinary consciousness and the perception of natural circumstances were withheld, and the soul was susceptible only to the vision imparted by God"; and, "ecstasy is a condition in which a person is so transported out of his natural state that he falls into a trance," a supernatural state wherein he may see visions in the spirit.

A trance is basically an ecstatic experience wherein one is more or less stupified, stunned. Herein he's susceptible only to the visions God would impart. If a trance, which is also known as a *deep sleep from the Lord,* occurs while the person is already asleep, any of the *visual* or *actual* kinds of supernatural dreams may be experienced. One may see visions, hear words (earthly or heavenly ones), or he may even leave his body and travel in the spirit for a special reason. Of course, these things are not to be self-induced, but experienced only as the Lord wills them. Otherwise we're out there without His protective armour.

When the great Apostle Peter drew near unto God by going up upon the housetop and praying, God drew near unto him and gave him this powerful vision:

Acts 10:9-16 On the morrow, as they went on their journey, and drew nigh unto the city, Peter went up upon the housetop to pray about the sixth hour: And he became very hungry, and would have eaten: but while they made ready, he fell into a trance, And saw heaven opened, and a certain vessel descending unto him, as it had been a great sheet knit at the four corners, and let down to the earth: Wherein were all manner of fourfooted beasts of the earth, and wild beasts, and creeping things, and fowls of the air. And there came a voice to him, Rise, Peter: kill, and eat. But Peter said, Not so, Lord; for I have never eaten any thing that is common or unclean. And the voice spake unto him again the second time, What God hath cleansed, that call not thou common. This was done thrice: and the vessel was received up again into heaven.

The voice speaking, and the symbols used, were familiar to Peter. But because the message jarred his tradition, God confirmed Himself again, and again, with the same vision. It was seen thrice, three times. God often confirms and reconfirms Himself when He speaks to us by supernatural means--especially when we're not fluent in communications divine. His will is that we become "family" with heavenly things--our citizenship, our "conversation," is up in that sphere, (Philippians 3:20). And if He wills, He can speak with us even as He spoke with His servants of old.

Balaam, a Gentile prophet of the Old Testament, also received a revelation from God in a trance, and blessed the Israelites:

Numbers 24:4 He hath said, which heard the words of God, which saw the vision of the Almighty, falling into a trance, but having his eyes open.

The Apostle Paul was likewise visited by Jesus while in prayer, and saw Him:

Acts 22:17-21 And it came to pass, that, when I was come again to Jerusalem, even while I prayed in the temple, I was in a trance; And saw Him saying unto me, Make haste, and get thee quickly out of Jerusalem: for they will not receive thy testimony concerning Me. And I said, Lord, they know that I imprisoned and beat in every synagogue them that believed on Thee: And when the blood of Thy martyr Stephen was shed, I also was standing by, and consenting unto his death, and kept the raiment of them that slew him. And He said unto me, Depart: for I will send thee far hence unto the Gentiles.

Paul here conversed supernaturally with Jesus Christ while in a trance. They communicated in words speakable because Paul remained in the earth during this experience. He wasn't beholding marvels in the Third Heaven as he did on another occasion.

While in his trance and seeing a vision from of the Lord, each of these men received an instructive revelation from the Lord which directly clarified his circumstance at that particular time, and pointed him to the will of God for that hour. Peter had been so busy preaching the Gospel and causing revival among the Jews that he neglected Christ's commission to preach the Gospel *in all the world, to every creature.* God had to define to him the Great Commission in a new light, in a supernatural way.

Balaam's vision was directly related to Israel's blessing and helped him to prophesy those blessings. It was God's time for those blessings to be spoken on Israel's behalf, and Balaam had made himself available to speak God's will, so God used him.

In great danger during persecution, the Apostle Paul desperately needed to know God's leading. In a trance while praying, he received the guidance and encouragement he needed. While in a trance, we may see and/or hear what is most prominent in our spirits and receive God's wisdom for our immediate situation.

While seeking the Lord in prayer some time ago, I'd been asking Him if I should preach less often on the buses and subways in New York City, where I live. At that time, I was persecuted and belittled for preaching in public. In prayer one night, the Lord took me in a trance. In its first stages, I saw myself in a vision preaching more fervently on the buses, for that had been on my heart for some days. Then the trance intensified, and the Lord blessed me in other ways too.

A couple of days later, I rode the bus again on my way to church, and I preached to the passengers. After a few minutes, the bus driver, and a drunkard, and some others began attacking me with words, and approached me to stop me. Deep in my spirit, I encouraged myself in the Lord, and continued preaching while ignoring their persecutions. I was determined to obey the heavenly vision I'd recently received in the trance. (Without that vision, I might have "perished" and not "prospered" in that work.)

After a few minutes, they all quieted down and backed off, and allowed me to go on preaching to them. I continued unceasingly as though I hadn't heard their complaints. Then I got off at my stop.

There are greater and lesser degrees of ecstatic experiences. One may "soar higher" or "see clearer" than another in visions and revelations when stunned by the "electrical touch" of God. I use the term "electrical touch" because it's very similar to the current of electricity. But it's not painful or tormenting. Rather, it is rapturous and delightful, as defined by Webster.

On the greater scale, one may be en-tranced into a profound spiritual sight and be literally, physically paralyzed for awhile by the Spirit of God as He communicates to him. It is truly one of the most life-changing experiences a person could ever have. On the lower level, one may simply be "caught by surprise" and be in awe or wonder. Or he may be excited in the Holy Ghost, amazed at a miracle or vision, or just joyful in the Lord.

Vine's Expository Dictionary Of New Testament Words also defines a trance (ecstasy) as "any displacement, and hence, especially, with reference to the mind, of that alteration of the normal condition by which the person is thrown into a state of surprise or fear, or both." The New Testament words "amazed," "amazement," and "astonishment," have also been translated from *ekstasis.*

This is what happened to the witnesses who saw Jesus raise the twelve-year-old damsel from the dead (Mark 5:42); to Mary Magdalene and others who were with her when an angel of God spoke to them of Jesus' resurrection (Mark 16:8); to the people in the temple who saw a lame man healed and praising God (Acts 3:10); and to those who witnessed Jesus forgive and heal a man who had the sickness palsy, (Luke 5:26).

In this latter case, the Greek rendering indicates that the people "were" ecstatic. The word *ekstasis* (here, "amazed) is used with the Greek word *lambano* ("were"), which means "to take, to get hold of, and to seize, as through effort." This same word, *lambano,* is used by Paul when he exhorts us to strive to "obtain" an incorruptible crown,

(1Corinthians 9:25).

Luke 5:24-26 But that ye may know that the Son of man hath power upon earth to forgive sins, (He said unto the sick of the palsy,) I say unto thee, Arise, and take up thy couch, and go into thine house. And immediately he rose up before them, and took up that whereon he lay, and departed to his own house, glorifying God. And they were all amazed, and they glorified God, and were filled with fear, saying, We have seen strange things today.

Of the people present here, some were amazed, others glorified God, and the rest were filled with fear. Those amazed were en-tranced into the spiritual realm where they were yielded and inclined to visions of God (although He probably didn't impart visions to all of them).

These people were havin' church! They had made an effort to come to Jesus' meeting. They came expecting healings and miracles and were gonna get theirs, if they had to break down the walls--and they did! (Talk about bringin' down da house!)

As the power of the Lord was present, they got ahold of the realm of the spirit and went into *ecstasy, (amazement, excitement, the beginning stages of stupefaction).* While in ecstasy, God could've easily communicated to them by supernatural revelation if He wanted to. Probably some of them were "slain in the spirit."

Clearly, we're to walk, even live, in the spirit, always acknowledging the Lord. And if the Spirit would bid us "Come up hither," we should have an ear to hear and an eye to see the vision He would impart. One can enter the spiritual dimension and see, hear, and even converse supernaturally therein.

If one allows fear to get ahold of him, God might back off and try another time, or another person. If he yields in faith with his mind and heart trusting in Jesus, there is no good thing which the Lord will withhold from him. It's His good pleasure to show us the things from above and to communicate extranaturally with us therefrom.

Many trances in the Bible are not specifically referred to as such. Yet the terms used, the contexts in which they're set, and the definitions of the original words, show us that God communicated via trances quite often. Here too, each experience may slightly differ. Recounting a supernatural trance which he experienced, the Prophet Daniel writes:

Daniel 10:7-9 And I Daniel alone saw the vision: for the men that were with me saw not the vision; but a *great quaking fell upon them,* so that they fled to hide themselves. Therefore I was left alone, and *saw* this great vision, and there remained *no strength* in me: for my comeliness was turned in me into *corruption,* and I retained *no strength.* Yet *heard* I the voice of His words: and when I heard the voice of His words, then was I in a *deep sleep* on my face, and my face toward the ground.

Daniel 10:7-9 (niv) I, Daniel, was the only one who saw the vision; the men with me did not see it, but such *terror overwhelmed them* that they fled and hid themselves. So I was left alone, *gazing* at this great vision; I had *no strength* left, my face turned *deathly pale* and I was *helpless.* Then *I heard* Him speaking, and as I listened to Him, I fell into a *deep sleep,* my face to the ground.

Daniel 10:7-9 (tev) I was the only one who saw the vision. The men who were with me did not see anything, but they were *terrified* and ran and hid. I was left there alone, *watching* this amazing vision. I had *no strength* left, and my face was so *changed* that no one could have recognized me. When I *heard* His voice, *I fell* to the ground *unconscious* and lay there face downward.   (All italics mine)

The Prophet Ezekiel said, "The hand of the Lord God fell there upon me," (Ezekiel 8:1); again, "Suddenly the power of the Sovereign Lord came on me," (Ezekiel 8:1 tev). Eliphaz said, "Fear came upon me, and trembling, which made all my bones to shake. Then a spirit passed before my face; the hair of my flesh stood up," (Job 4:14-15). John said, "And when I saw Him (Jesus) I fell at His feet as dead," (Revelation 1:17).

As we saw with Abraham, with Jacob, and with Daniel, many of these experiences astonished and even troubled those who received them. The immediate effect that supernatural experiences can have upon us can be quite impactful and sobering. Trances have occasionally been the cause of the rethinking of matters and the reordering of many lives and ministries.

Trances can also bless our souls, and our bodies as well, with a most wonderful anointing or presence from God. A cleansed, refreshed, and revived body and spirit, and an intense closeness to Jesus, are usual results of a trance. So we see that a much greater realm than the natural exists, and that a whole world of possible spiritual revelations and experiences from God is available.

We may have a supernatural experience from the Lord, perhaps visit the Third Heaven and return, and be endued with power from on high! Many people who have had trances, gone to Heaven, or seen Jesus or an angel, testify that during their experience God anointed them with more gifts of the Spirit, more of the fruit of the Spirit (the character of Christ), more wisdom, or more of something else from God. At times, they didn't even realize at first that they had been anointed in a special way. But after awhile they began to see new things, new gifts, or a greater anointing, operating in their lives and ministries. God may commission us anew in supernatural experiences, so it is likely He will also empower us anew to go forth.

The trance comes in a matter of moments, usually, not in a fraction of a second, and not slowly and waveringly. It has also been known to come "suddenly." It may begin with the same experience you're already familiar with when enjoying the presence of the Lord (such as Holy Ghost "goose bumps," fire, joy, etc.), and then the Lord will take you further. You may be standing, sitting, prostrate, or on your back. Your eyes may be open, or closed. Your arms my be lifted, or relaxed at your sides. It may occur while you're in church, at home in private prayer, or even while you're sleeping--or for that matter, anywhere and anytime. God is God!

But it will always bring a blessing, a confirmation, a direction, a refreshing, a healing, an exhortation, an instruction, an illumination, an enduement of power, or something else from God. He visits always with a purpose. And what He shows us in a trance may be visions of the highest, Paradisal Heaven, or of the lower, stellar heavens, or of the lowest, atmospheric sky. He might want us to see heavenly things, or earthly goings-on. But remember, it's always up to Him.

2Corinthians 12:1-4 It is not expedient for me doubtless to glory. I will come to visions and revelations of the Lord. I knew a man in Christ above fourteen years ago, (whether in the body, I cannot tell; or whether out of the body, I cannot tell; God knoweth;) such an one caught up to the Third Heaven. And I knew such a man, (whether in the body, or out of the body, I cannot tell: God knoweth;) How that he was caught up into Paradise, and heard unspeakable words, which it is not lawful for a man to utter.

Here, the Apostle Paul relates a supernatural experience he'd had over fourteen years earlier. He knew a man, doubtless himself, who soared in the heavens and reached the Third Heaven, the Abode of God. He'd been summoned up Thither by the Spirit of the Lord. Emphasizing that he didn't know if he was in his physical body, he shows us that the spirit of a man has a form like his body, and also has tangibility--hence his inability to make a distinction between them.

Words unspeakable (too sacred to utter) he was privileged to hear, though not to communicate in the earth. Brethren, we often too casually confess a desire to see visions and to enjoy supernatural experiences. We ought honestly to consider Paul's humble reluctance to share this experience. (He did so for the need of the Corinthian Christians--and then fourteen years after it happened.) Highly learned and skilled in the words of Holy Scripture, and ordained in the highest office of the Christian ministry, we might expect he'd come back with a full report, a message, an observation at least; but no--speechless.

Let's observe that even the greatest minds cannot comprehend the things from over There unless God opens our understanding to them. Observe also that the experience was not completely foreign to Paul either--from his conversion he'd had spectacular doings with the sky.

As a rule, when God speaks or reveals something to us by visions, dreams, or other supernatural means, the message and its form will not be completely foreign to us. There will usually be something familiar to us in it which we're to recognize and follow until we see our Jesus and the message He would impart. And if He is pleased to utter the unlawful, we marvel.

We also need to understand that when God gives us a supernatural experience it is not necessarily an endorsement of our denomination, doctrine, or lifestyle. Sometimes signs and wonders are intended as an incitement for us to go on to perfection, such as when an angel from God directed Cornelius to Peter so that he would be born-again and filled with the Holy Ghost, (Acts 10). Although Cornelius was a holy and devout man, he was bound by religious tradition and needed to come to the knowledge of the truth.

Christians of greatly differing denominations, doctrines, and lifestyles, have since the Early Church Period experienced supernatural revelations and manifestations of the Spirit of God. Yet they would often remain divided in purpose and in the practise of their faith. Obviously God, the Author of Peace, doesn't smile upon the division which exists between the various Christian groups. But it pleases Him to bless and use His people with power. He's not quick to repent of His call upon our lives and to remove His anointing from us, (Romans 11:29).

In some instances, divine manifestations of God may indeed endorse certain areas of our lives--they may testify of His blessing upon our lives. Such was the case when the Heavenly Father told Jesus, "In Thee I am *well pleased,"* when the Holy Spirit appeared as a Dove at His baptism, (Luke 3:22). When the archangel Gabriel visited the virgin Mary, he called her *highly favoured* of God, and *blessed* among women (Luke 1:28), and he called Daniel a man *greatly beloved* when he visited him, (Daniel 10:11).

There are many benefits brought about by special manifestations of God. They can confirm God's presence in our lives, and give us confidence in His will. They can correct us from error, and lead us to truth. They can deliver us from any obstacles, and empower us for service. There's nothing we can need which God's supernatural presence can't provide. And when there's absolutely no way in this natural world for a matter to be worked out, a way can always be made in the supernatural. "God specializes in things thought impossible."

Luke 1:37   For with God nothing shall be impossible.

Supernatural experiences also help to promote unity and purity of ministry. Being a non-Jew, Cornelius was not permitted to be in fellowship with Peter and other Jews, according to Old Testament law. But the angelic leading resulted in the unity of the faith of Jesus Christ--among Jews and Gentiles--according to New Testament grace.

No matter how spectacular, astonishing, or glorious a supernatural experience may be, we may desire and ask God for them, only not casually or presumptuously. He doesn't tell us not to seek spiritual things or approach unto them. He doesn't tell us that they're dangerous and should be avoided because the devil might try to deceive us by coming to us an an angel of light. We know we have an enemy. But we cannot stop seeking the things of God just because the devil might try to deceive us.

The Bible says, "Look up" (Luke 21:28); "Seek those things which are above" (Colossians 3:1); and "If you see Me, you shall be anointed; but if not, it shall not be so," (2Kings 2:10 author's paraphrase). Evidently these verses indicate that we've got to yield ourselves unto the Lord by faith, believing He will respond to us. Certainly we're supposed to walk primarily by faith, and not by sights, (2Corinthians 5:7). But we do have the biblical right to ask and expect supernatural visitations of God.

The Bible abounds with accounts of people seeking supernatural demonstrations of God. Manoah, Samson's father, asked God to show him an angel, and God granted his request, (Judges 13:8). Elisha prayed asking God to open his servant's spiritual eyes so that he would be able to see the angels in the realm of the spirit, and God did it, (2Kings 6:17). Daniel asked God for a supernatural revelation concerning a dream, and the Lord answered him--in another dream, (Daniel 2:17-19).

The Prophet Joel said that God's people will prophesy in the last days and as a result there will be, among other things, manifestations of dreams and visions, (Joel 2:28). A multitude of Christians asked God for manifestations of signs and wonders, and He answered, (Acts 4:29-30).

Paul said, "I will come to visions and revelations of the Lord," (2Corinthians 12:1b). The Greek word *boulomai,* which is translated "will" here, means "volition, intention, purpose, and determination," according to *Strong's Exhaustive Concordance.* It also means "deliberate design, desire, inclination, and option," according to *Vine's Expository Dictionary.*

As a matter of choice, by an act of my will, I incline to dreams, visions, trances, angelic visitations, and any other supernatural experiences of the Lord which he chooses to give me, (if and when He so chooses). I don't attempt these things on my own, but I choose to incline and yield to them when that's the way He's moving.

We must obey God when He says, "Draw near unto Me, and I will draw near unto you," (James 4:8a). With a basic knowledge of the Word of God and of the supernatural workings of Him, and with some faith, we'll not only be able to discern the spirits whether they are of God when we draw near unto the Lord, but we'll also be able to enjoy the things which are Above.

Colossians 3:1-2 If ye then be risen with Christ, seek those things which are above, where Christ sitteth on the right hand of God. Set your affection on things above, not on things on the earth.

Let's seek first the Kingdom of God. And let's desire a better country, that is, an heavenly. Paul said our conversation is in Heaven, so living in the supernatural realm should be natural for Christians.

If a son asks something good of his natural father, he'll give it to him. He won't give him something bad, (Luke 11:9-13). How much more shall our Heavenly Father give good things from that Heavenly City He's prepared for us? God will not disappoint us with manifestations of the devil when we ask for manifestations of Him. In the Holy Bible, when God's angels visited His servants, they usually told them, "Fear not." We too should not fear, but in faith welcome supernatural manifestations.

We shouldn't inquire into the supernatural realm presumptuously. Neither should we draw back therefrom because of fear. We should trust God with the same spirit of faith His servants in the Bible had, and welcome the same kinds of experiences they enjoyed. God desires to visit and bless His people ever-so-wonderfully through supernatural experiences--day ones and night ones--if only we would yield to Him in faith.

During the time of this writing, I dreamed that I was travelling in the spirit in an out-of-body experience. I saw several angels descending into my neighbourhood and visiting a young Christian lady to bless her somehow as she slept. I believe that she symbolically represented the spiritually young ones in the Body of Christ. Although at the same time, she might also have been an actual person.

These supernatural beings didn't have wings or special garments to show that they were angels of God. Some angels have wings and some do not. So I had to use the knowledge and discernment I'd gained to "try" these celestial beings and determine whether they were of God. I soon discerned they were of God.

As they visited the young lady, they began to take her up in the spirit hoping she would welcome and yield to their visit. But she began to think that she was either being visited by evil angels, or by beings from another planet, or that she was having a bad dream. I tried urging her not to fear, saying, "These are angels of God coming to bless you." But she became so afraid that she "willed" herself out of that realm and back into natural sleep, and awakened without that special blessing. Sadly, the angels then, unable to impart the blessing, left airward.

From this I understand that the Body of Christ often misses God's blessings because they come in ways that are new and unfamiliar to us. Unlike Peter, we too often stay in the boat when Jesus comes to us in a new way and says, "It is I, be not afraid." If His coming unto us was always the same, we wouldn't require faith to receive Him. But there are always new things with Him, and without faith it is impossible to please Him, (Hebrews 11:6).

Not without a holy fear and trembling, let us seek those things which are Above, where Christ sits on the right hand of God, and set our affection on them. In this way practising for the Rapture, when we'll go up "body and all" (and know it!), we may learn how to boldly approach the Throne of Grace and enjoy our citizenship in Heaven.

A Prophecy (May 5, 1989)

"Thus saith the Lord, truly I am pouring out of My Spirit in these last days as never before. As I spoke to My servant Joel many centuries ago, visions and dreams are abounding in this time because these are the very last of the last days. My people, you're gonna need to know by supernatural revelation what I am doing in this last hour, and where I want each one.

I'm visiting many of My people personally, saith the Lord, and I'm also sending My angels to guard and guide not only the saints, but also them who shall be heirs of salvation. Many people are seeing these angels--in visions, in dreams, and in circumstances. Watch, and pray, that you too may behold My moving, saith the Lord, for I truly am moving by My Spirit. Enter into spiritual things, for they are given unto thee to enjoy. You should feel at home in the realm of the spirit.

I'll keep nothing hidden from those who seek Me in spirit and in truth. That which has been reserved for the last hour of this Age has been released, saith the Lord, for this is the last hour. That which the prophets have prophesied of, and the intercessors have prayed for, and the teachers have taught about, is here--you're in it.

So come, come ye to the waters, even into the deep, for the deep has been given unto thee. The heavens, yea, even the Third Heaven, is open now and welcomes whosoever will yield in faith to see Me. Do you have faith? Yes, even now the gift of faith for the supernatural, eyes to see, even child-like faith, are imparted unto you, My people. I have blessings from Heaven for all My people, and I would not have anyone to miss his portion.

That which I would show and give thee by above-natural means, saith the Lord, you don't want to miss. You're going to need My enduements of powers from Above for the tasks yet ahead. I work a work in these last days which will not lack supernatural armament and strategy within My Army. I'm setting things aright in the earth. All things are under My control. I'm revealing secrets. A Glorious Church is being prepared for a marriage in the sky. In a moment, in the twinkling of an eye, You'll be caught up to be with Me.

So go on, work on, preach on, hope on, for your labour is not in vain, and your redemption is near. I've won the war against evil, and I have given you the victory--no weapon formed against you shall prosper. Rejoice, for I've saved the best for last, saith the Lord of Hosts, and Satan doesn't know what I'm about to do. Rejoice because you have the victory, victories are being given unto My Body, and the greatest victory of the Age, the Catching Away of the Church, is coming on the horizon, saith the Lord."

Chapter 9

End-Time Dreamers

Daniel 1:17   Daniel had understanding
in all visions and dreams.

Daniel 5:11-12 There is a man in thy kingdom, in whom is the Spirit of the holy gods; and in the days of thy father light and understanding and wisdom, like the wisdom of the gods, was found in him; whom the king Nebuchadnezzar thy father, the king, I say, thy father, made master of the magicians, astrologers, Chaldeans, and soothsayers; Forasmuch as an excellent spirit, and knowledge, and understanding, interpreting of dreams, and showing of hard sentences, and dissolving of doubts, were found in the same Daniel, whom the king named Belteshazzar: now let Daniel be called, and he will shew the interpretation.

All people dream, Christians and sinners alike. Most dreams are not remembered, and fewer yet are understood. To help us interpret our dreams and receive messages from God, the Holy Spirit distributes various gifts to some of His servants. To one is given *divers kinds of dreams,* to another *the interpretation of dreams.*

Daniel 1:17 As for these four children, God gave them knowledge and skill in all learning and wisdom: and Daniel had understanding in all visions and dreams.

Daniel was peculiarly gifted in the area of dreams, interpretations, understandings, and the like. His "excellent spirit" received and brought forth great revelations from God. So profound were some of his visions and dreams that angels from the Third Heaven, including the archangel Gabriel himself, have personally visited him to communicate the interpretations.

On one occasion, after much prayer, it was disclosed to Daniel in a dream what King Nebuchadnezzar of Babylon had dreamed. He also received the interpretation of that dream from God. These secrets in the king's subconscious mind were revealed supernaturally. We should understand here, though, that this was a matter of life and death. Had his dream and its interpretation not been revealed to the king by Daniel's intercessions and insights, he would have destroyed all of his counsellors out of anger--including Daniel and his brethren.

I don't think that in an ordinary situation a person should see if he can guess what someone else has dreamed. This may be a form of tempting God, or of playing with His Spirit. In serious matters, such as Daniel's life-threatening circumstance, God can and will reveal secrets which are otherwise unfathomable.

There aren't many men like Daniel today, but there are some--servants and handmaidens of God used greatly in dreaming dreams. Some are more anointed than others. Some may dream more, others may interpret more. But though one might not be anointed in these areas like Daniel was, he may still enjoy dreams from the Lord. All Christians are born of God, and He gives all of us dreams born of His Spirit.

We may ask the Lord to use us in this area for His glory. If we are called to a high office in the Christian ministry, He may anoint us more powerfully. But even if we're not, He may still be pleased to give us the gifts of His Holy Spirit. He's looking for people who are willing to be used in His service in these end-times.

The anointings for dreaming dreams of God and for the interpreting of dreams can be imparted in several ways. God's anointed servants can lay hands on a person and prayerfully impart the gifts God would endue him with. In private prayer, one can ask for and receive these gifts directly from God. By studying about dreams and dreaming according to the Bible, one's mind can be renewed and his spirit equipped to dream dreams inspired of the Holy Spirit.

The corporate anointing of God's presence in the Church can also impart these gifts upon God's people. A corporate atmosphere of faith for supernatural anointings greatly enhances them. We must learn to yield, and teach others and help them yield, to all movings of the Spirit, both super and simple ones. Then when He desires to anoint us we won't grieve Him.

When the anointing is upon me, after a powerful church service or after prayer, I usually have greater dreams. I generally dream dreams from the Lord all the time, but I have found in my experience that when I'm in the spirit my dreams are more supernatural, more directly ordered of the Lord. Praying with the spirit in other tongues makes me more spiritually-minded, hence more conducive to revelations of the Spirit. Therefore, I pray in tongues before going to sleep, often for two or three hours, and always receive dreams from the Lord as a result.

For awhile, I had neglected praying before bedtime and the presence of God in my dreams began to lessen. Then I prayed in tongues for about three hours one night, and as I slept throughout that night, my mind was flooded with a great heavenly light. I was very yielded to Jesus, and if He had something to say, I had ears to hear--or, a mind to dream.

I have gone to sleep after little or no prayer and still received dreams from the Lord, even the supernatural kinds. The greater kinds of dreams have usually come when I was in the spirit. However, the Lord, Who is sovereign, has visited me in dreams when I was not in the spirit. We are more yielded to revelations from God when we are in the spirit, but they are still given as He wills.

If I seem to stress speaking with other tongues, it is because the New Testament does so. In the Early Church, the experience of being baptized in the Holy Ghost with the evidence of speaking with other tongues as the Spirit gave utterance often occurred simultaneously with being born-again, (Acts 10:44-46). This shows us how important it was, and still is, to speak with other tongues. Praying with all kinds of prayer, including with other tongues, is to be practised always, (Ephesians 6:18).

If a Christian loves the Lord but doesn't speak with other tongues, he should ask the Lord to baptize Him in the Spirit, yield his tongue to Him in prayer, and commence to speak with tongues by faith. It will be done according to his faith, and the anointing of God's presence will manifest in confirmation that it is of God. The Lord communicates to us on our level of prayer, but the importance of praying with the help of the Holy Spirit, in His own language, cannot be over-emphasized. And He always wants us progressing in our levels of prayer.

(Important as it is to speak with other tongues, a person can still be born-again, saved, anointed, and used in God's service, even if he doesn't speak with other tongues.)

At times I know when I'm going to have a special dream. One night, I knew a special message from God was coming in a dream. Throughout that night I awakened several times after dreaming. Each time I said to myself, "That's not it." Finally it came--a special message I knew was due me that night.

On another occasion, I'd dreamed a dream with symbols and didn't understand it. Throughout that night I tossed and turned in my sleep asking the Lord for the interpretation. It came before morning--in another dream! The message came in one dream, and its interpretation came in another.

Before writing this book, I had many study notes on various Bible topics. I had already begun taperecording some of my teachings, but felt I should write a book. I began asking the Lord in prayer what I should write about, though I had already written four small booklets which supplemented some of the taped teaching series. One of the series, with a blue-colored booklet, is entitled, "DREAMS: Understanding the Visions of the Night and Their Interpretations."

Somehow I had believed that God would tell me what to write about in a dream. Soon afterward I saw the blue-colored booklet about "DREAMS" in a dream. Except for the cover color and design, there was no other detail or message in that dream. I believe God was answering me, saying that this is what He wanted me to write about. I immediately thereafter began to organize my notes and write this book. And during the time of this project, I have enjoyed several more dreams from God about it.

Sometimes before going to sleep I sense an angelic presence. God's angels are always ministering for me (and for all Christians too), and I always acknowledge their presence by faith. But sometimes their presence takes on an especially active, energetic sense, even in the night seasons. I then know I'm going to experience a supernatural dream, a trance, an angelic visitation, the audible voice of the Lord, or something else of that calibre. By knowing it's going to happen before it does, I'm in a position to prepare for it.

We can prepare ourselves for a supernatural experience by binding the devil who might attempt to hinder it, by loosing the angels who minister for us in it, by yielding our spirits to it in faith, and by welcoming the Holy Spirit and letting Him have His way. Yet we won't always know in advance what's to come.

Supernatural experiences are given as the Spirit of God wills, not as we will (1Corinthians 12:11), and He may choose to come upon us "suddenly," (as in Acts 2:1-4). We should determine to make ourselves conducive to supernatural experiences by being spiritually-minded all the time. This way, having prepared the way of the Lord, we'll be fit for His coming and prepared unto every good blessing, or, prepared for every good dream.

Everyone can receive dreams and visions of the Lord, and in these end-times many will, (Joel 2:28). But many will not receive those of the spectacular sort. The gifts and callings of God may differ greatly among individuals. One may be more gifted in spiritual matters, and another in business and organizational matters.

Let's not despise or decry our brother's or our sister's gift simply because it differs from ours. "If the whole body were an eye, where were the hearing?" (1Corinthians 12:12-27). We are many members in particular, yet but one Body of Christ, and have been all made to drink into one Spirit.

1Corinthians 12:11 (amp) All these [achievements and abilities] are inspired and brought to pass by One and the same (Holy) Spirit, Who apportions to each person individually [exactly] as He chooses.

Now there are diversities of gifts, but the same Spirit, and He distributes to every man his own, as He chooses. It must be understood that "each individual person" in verse 11 means every *Christian* person. The gifts of the Holy Spirit are given only to those who are baptized into Him in the new birth--that is, those who are born-again. It is not for non-Christians to know or be endued with the powers of God. But unto His Church it is given in the behalf of Christ, not only to believe on Him, but to be gifted of Him.

During the time of this writing, I dreamed that I was teaching about dreams to a body of believers--only many of them weren't believing me. I discerned that one of the congregants was not a Christian, and that he was involved in some form of eastern mysticism and meditation. He intently listened to what I was teaching, hoping to tap into some of the spiritual truths I was sharing. The Christians were not paying attention to me, but instead murmured that my words were unfamiliar and unconventional.

From this dream, I understand that many Christians fear new revelations, fresh manna. The ungodly are sometimes more daring and courageous to receive spiritual knowledge than we to whom it really belongs. Yet when one is willing to receive the knowledge of God, great deliverance and great blessing can follow.

Soon after that dream, I dreamed a very encouraging dream. Someone asked me to pray for a little girl who had been suffering from an extreme case of nightmares. Other attempts at healing were unsuccessful, but through prayer the power of God set her free. Hallelujah!

From this dream, I understand that the power of God can set the captives free, and that God will use me to bless others. And I also understand that babes in Christ, new Christians, are sometimes more yielded to the Spirit of God than older Christians--they're not as much set in their ways.

Jesus has many things to say unto us, and to do for us. But many people are still not able to bear His words (John

16:12), to eat strong meat (Hebrews 5:14), to turn the key of knowledge (Matthew 16:19), to know the things that are freely given to us of God, (1Corinthians 2:12).

But this is the time of the end of all things. The Book is no longer sealed, (Daniel 12:4). The Holy Spirit has been sent to guide us into all truth and set us free, (John 8:31-32; 16:13-15). We need only to have "hearing ears" and receptive hearts.

My prayer is that the reader would be enlightened, delivered, and anointed to dream godly dreams. By the anointing of God, by knowledge, and by faith in these words, a new spiritual dimension has been disclosed--the realm of dreaming.

"Heavenly Father, I pray that You would give Your people a sound understanding according to truth in the area of dreams and visions. Restore in us a special faith to live in the spirit and move boldly and skillfully in that realm, where You are, Lord. I pray these words would prosper whereto You send them, and that they would multiply and produce fruit unto You in many lives. May You anoint again those who with eyes of faith would see You here.

Confirm Yourself, Lord, unto Your people, with signs and wonders and visions and dreams of the Holy Ghost. I believe that many supernatural anointings are coming upon and enduing Your people right now for blessing, for healing, and for service, through these words You have given through Your servant. I thank You for it, Lord God, and give You all the glory, honour, and praise. In Jesus' holy, mighty, and precious Name, I pray. Amen."

Glossary

The following words are defined according to the author's special usage in this book, and do not necessarily reflect conventional dictionary definitions.

actual   A dream or vision in which the person's spirit is actively participating in some way. This may or may not be a supernatural experience, depending mostly on the degree of God's presence in and ordering of it.

angels   Supernatural beings created by God to serve Him in many ways, both in Heaven, and on earth. Many of them function as messengers of righteousness to men, and they are invisible, powerful, and good. There are also evil angels, such as Satan, who fell from grace.

anointing   The tangible anointing of the Holy Spirit. He can visit us in a great variety of ways and for a great variety of reasons, but it is the anointing of His presence when we can see, hear, feel, or otherwise know that He is manifesting Himself in a literal way.

audible   Sounds or words in the spiritual realm which are clearly heard by the external, physical ear, or by the internal, spiritual ear. It is more supernatural than the still, small voice of the Holy Spirit in that it is louder and more vibrant.

body   The physical body with all its senses and functions; the "earth-suit" we were born into this world in and shall put off when we die. It is often a major participant in supernatural experiences.

Body of Christ   The universal Church of God over which Jesus Christ is Lord. The united, collective family of God, made up of every true born-again Christian, whatever Christian church he may be a part of.

Christian   A person who has accepted Jesus Christ as his own personal Lord and Saviour. A born-again child of the living God whose sins have been washed away by the precious Blood of the Lamb of God, (Revelation 1:5).

consciousness   The normal mental state of awareness which we experience while we are awake, and which abates when we are asleep.

deep sleep   A deep state of natural sleep, or a deep state of supernatural sleep. Godly dreams can occur in either state, but the latter kind is directly caused by the Lord and is the same thing as a trance.

deliverance   This is a process of being set free from the oppressing power of evil spirits. It is accomplished by the power of the Holy Spirit as the person desires and cooperates with His help. The Lord may use a person to minister deliverance to another person, or He may minister it Himself. It may be a gradual process, or it may occur instantaneously.

demons   A class of evil spirits. Disembodied spirits who roam the earth seeking to enter and oppress people. These are different from fallen angels, which followed Satan's rebellion in the heavens and are in his class of being.

dream   Also known as a vision of the night, this is a message produced in the mind while the person is sleeping. Both good and evil thoughts and ideas--intelligible ones or unintelligible ones--can arise from the subconscious. The more that God is inspiring a dream, the more supernatural (above the natural plane) the dream is.

gifts of the Spirit   These are special enduements of the Holy Spirit which manifest as He wills. They have nothing to do with natural talent or ability. There are nine specific gifts, and they can operate only in Christians.

God's Word   The Holy Bible, God's written Word, which includes 39 Old Testament books and 27 New Testament books. In this study, we refer to God's Word in four different versions: King James Version, New International Version (niv), Today's English Version (tev), and the Amplified Bible (amp).

impression   A perception of the inner man of the heart. A feeling, prompting, hunch, thought, or idea, which the Lord impresses upon the spiritual senses. It is the most common and basic form of communication which the Holy Spirit uses in His speaking to us. Impressions require spiritual sensitivity and discernment in order to be accurately perceived, and are therefore often misinterpreted or missed.

interpretation   The understood meaning of a message which has been revealed in a dream or other kind of vision. Most revelations contain symbols, and can be interpreted only as the symbols are properly understood.

mind   The emotional and intellectual faculties of a person. Although the physical and spiritual parts of man play a role in dreams and visions, his mind has the most important role because it is there that he perceives the message, interprets it, and it is there that his will must decide whether or not to obey it.

other tongues   A personal, spiritual prayer language which Christians can employ. By speaking with other tongues, we may speak unto God with words which cannot be articulated in our regular earthly kind of speech. It is our spirit praying to Him in His own way and by His own help, (1Corinthians 14:2).

out-of-body experience   An operation of the Holy Spirit in which a person's spirit leaves his body and travels in the spiritual realm. He may stay within the borders of the earth's atmosphere (the first heaven), or go into outer space (the second heaven), or even go to the Paradise of God, (the Third Heaven). As is true of all supernatural experiences, this should be directly initiated by the Lord, and not self-induced.

presence   A distinct sense that a spiritual being (a good one or an evil one) is near us, even though we may not see or hear him. At times we can literally feel him on the physical body and even locate exactly where he is and what he is doing, as when a seraphim touched Isaiah's mouth with a live coal, (Isaiah 6:6-7).

revelation   A message from the Lord in a dream, vision, or prophecy. It contains truth inspired supernaturally, and it can affect the person in potentially powerful ways. By study and prayer, we may also have simpler revelations.

rhema   A Greek word indicating a revelation from the Lord such as a prophecy, vision, or dream, which shows His specific thoughts and leading personalized for a current situation to a particular individual or group. It is *the Word of God made alive in the now* (that is, *the prophetic word of the Lord).*

sinner   A person who has not accepted Jesus Christ as his own personal Lord and Saviour. Everyone is a lost sinner by nature until he accepts Jesus and repents of his sins, though he may be a nice person and a religious church-goer. And those who do belong to Christ are no longer sinners, even if they commit sins, because being in Christ, they are now partakers of the divine nature of God, (2Peter 1:4).

sleep   A normal, regularly recurring state of uncon-sciousness in which the physical body is at rest. The average person sleeps about eight hours each day, and it is then that he may dream.

spirit   This is the true essence of a being, the person he is inwardly. God is a "Spirit" (in this book, always capitalized), man is a spirit, angels are spirits, and demons are spirits. The inner character of a human being involves the fruit of their spirit, which the Apostle Paul speaks of in Galatians 5:19-23. A born-again Christian has the Christ-like nature in his spirit, and a non-Christian has the sinful nature in his spirit. Many people do not manifest in their real life their true spiritual nature, whatever it may be.

spiritual realm   This is the spiritual dimension where all spirits operate and all supernatural experiences originate. Everybody has contact with the spiritual realm all the time, whether or not they realize or believe in it. God is a Spirit and the Father of all spirits, (Hebrews 12:9). We all live and move and have our being in Him, (Acts 17:28).

subconscious   The great reservoir of mental and spiritual activity which functions mostly without our being aware of it. It involves our instincts, emotions, memories, self-concept, and other thought processes. It is our information source in natural dreams, and may be a gateway or avenue for supernatural dreams.

supernatural   The Greek word *pneumatikos* means "spiritual, above-the-natural, other-than-natural, and supernatural." A supernatural experience is one inspired by a power other than a natural one, and is manifested in some visible, audible, and/or tangible way.

supernatural dream   A dream directly inspired, ordered by the Lord. There are many degrees of the supernatural, and many kinds and levels of supernatural dreams. When God shows you things in dreams which you did not know naturally, or when you hear an audible voice during sleep, or when an angel of the Lord appears to you in a night vision, or when God anoints you with spiritual gifts as you sleep, it is a supernatural dream. It is akin to a trance.

symbol   This is a specific detail representing something else in a dream or vision. Bread, for example, can be a symbol of the Word of God, unless it means literal bread.

tangible   A quality of experience involving the physical senses. The emotions can affect the physical body in a tangible way in response to any type of vision. The greater kinds of visions can more greatly affect the body in a tangible way--irrespective of the person's emotional response. Trances can manifest tangibly so that not only a person's spiritual and mental awareness of their environment is altered, but also their respiration, pulse rate, and facial expression can be altered.

trance   A supernatural state of ecstasy in which the Holy Spirit tangibly comes upon a person and his perceptions are arrested and fully subjected to the will of God. In a low-level trance, they may retain a degree of normalcy. Trances may be used by the Lord as a gateway to other supernatural experiences, such as miracles, prophecies, visions, audible voices, and angelic activity.

vision   A sight supernaturally disclosed to the spiritual eyes. Sometimes the physical eyes partake in supernatural visions, as in the case of an actual angelic appearance. Many of the principles involved in the function, interpretation, and application of dreams, apply to those of visions because they are all in the same family of revelations.

visual   A dream or vision shown in the mind of the person, without his spirit participating actively in it. This may or may not be a supernatural revelation, depending on how inspired and ordered of God it is.

Bibliography

The Holy Bible, King James Version

The Holy Bible, New International Version (niv)
International Bible Society

The Holy Bible, Today's English Version (tev)
American Bible Society

The Amplified Bible Old Testament (amp)
Zondervan Corporation

The Amplified New Testament (amp)
Lockman Foundation

Webster's Unabridged Dictionary
William Collins and World Publishing Co., Inc.

Strong's Exhaustive Concordance of the Bible
Strong, James, Abingdon Press, New York

Vines Expository Dictionary of New Testament Words
Vine, W.E., Fleming H. Revell Co.,
Old Tappan, New Jersey

Index of Scripture References in Book Order
(Verse *references* are parenthesized, *quotations* are not)

Chapter 3

Chapter 4

Index of Scripture References in Biblical Order
(Verse *references* are parenthesized, *quotations* are not)

Index of Subjects